DATE DUE 5/09

GAYLORD			PRINTED IN U.S.A.

One Big Happy Family

by Rebecca Walker

Black, White & Jewish: Autobiography of a Shifting Self

Baby Love: Choosing Motherhood After a Lifetime of Ambivalence

edited by Rebecca Walker

To Be Real: Telling the Truth and Changing the Face of Feminism

What Makes a Man: 22 Writers Imagine the Future

One Big Happy Family 18 Writers

Talk About Polyamory, Open Adoption, Mixed Marriage, Househusbandry, Single Motherhood, and Other Realities of Truly Modern Love

edited and with an introduction by **Rebecca Walker**

Riverhead Books a member of Penguin Group (USA) Inc. NEW YORK 2009

RIVERHEAD BOOKS
Published by the Penguin Group
Penguin Group (USA) Inc., 375 Hudson Street, New York, New York 10014, USA • Penguin
Group (Canada), 90 Eglinton Avenue East, Suite 700, Toronto, Ontario M4P 2Y3, Canada
(a division of Pearson Canada Inc.) • Penguin Books Ltd, 80 Strand, London WC2R 0RL,
England • Penguin Ireland, 25 St Stephen's Green, Dublin 2, Ireland (a division of Penguin Books
Ltd) • Penguin Group (Australia), 250 Camberwell Road, Camberwell, Victoria 3124,
Australia (a division of Pearson Australia Group Pty Ltd) • Penguin Books India Pvt Ltd,
11 Community Centre, Panchsheel Park, New Delhi–110 017, India • Penguin Group (NZ),
67 Apollo Drive, Rosedale, North Shore 0632, New Zealand (a division of Pearson
New Zealand Ltd) • Penguin Books (South Africa) (Pty) Ltd, 24 Sturdee Avenue,
Rosebank, Johannesburg 2196, South Africa

Penguin Books Ltd, Registered Offices: 80 Strand, London WC2R 0RL, England

Page 257 constitutes an extension of this copyright page.

Library of Congress Cataloging-in-Publication Data

One big happy family : 18 writers talk about polyamory, open adoption, mixed marriage,
househusbandry, single motherhood, and other realities of truly modern love / edited and with an
introduction by Rebecca Walker.
    p.   cm.
    ISBN 978-1-59448-862-7
1. Family—United States.   2. Social values—United States.   I. Walker, Rebecca, date.
    HQ734.O64   2009   2008050339
    306.850973—dc22

Printed in the United States of America
10 9 8 7 6 5 4 3 2 1

Book design by Gretchen Achilles

While the author has made every effort to provide accurate telephone numbers and Internet
addresses at the time of publication, neither the publisher nor the author assumes any responsibility
for errors, or for changes that occur after publication. Further, the publisher does not have any
control over and does not assume any responsibility for author or third-party websites or their
content.

Contents

Introduction

For as long as I can remember, I've been fascinated by other people's families. My own family was fragmented and haunted by unfulfilled longings. My parents came from different races. They divorced. They began relationships with others. They had children with others. They lived three thousand miles apart. They had wildly divergent worldviews. They did not communicate often or, from my perspective, well. As I shuttled back and forth across the country to spend time with each parent, navigated the murky waters of a multiracial identity, and struggled to negotiate tricky relationships with my stepmother and half-siblings, I didn't feel my parents were fully aware of the implications of their decisions. Though they may have tried, they weren't able to ensure my emotional well-being in the midst of their vicissitudes. My parents loved each other deeply, but they never figured out how to actually be a family.

I can't say for sure why this was so. My parents both came from less than idyllic families, which may have had something to do with their difficulty charting a steadier course for ours. But my parents were also part of a larger generational movement that rebelled against the traditional nuclear family.

When they met in the early 1960s, divorce was stigmatized and not easy to obtain. Interracial marriage was illegal in most states, birth control just barely available, and abortion hidden away in back alleys. Women were just beginning to enter the workforce in large numbers. Homosexuality was classified as deviant, a psychiatric disorder. A family was expected to live in one community, in one house, for decades. Their children attended the local public or parochial school. Emotional subtleties were regarded with suspicion, and circumscribed "family values" went, for the most part, unquestioned.

Though you'd have to ask them for particulars, I think it's safe to say that my parents identified this paradigm as part of a larger system responsible for the oppression of women and people of color, and the repression of human sexuality and potential overall. Thus armed, they gave themselves permission to smash the paradigm to bits by doing the exact opposite of what was expected, which translated loosely into doing whatever they wanted or, perhaps more accurately, whatever they could piece together. This meant marrying when it was illegal to do so, cultivating both of their careers, and moving from one city to another as opportunities arose. It also meant divorcing without lawyers or acrimony, devising a custody plan that moved me between their houses, three thousand miles and many worlds apart, every two years. It meant not talking to each other for more than ten minutes, up until the day I graduated from high school.

Whether this chain of events transpired by happenstance or design, the result was the same. Plans were made, and then abandoned. Subsequent complications were left largely unresolved. I floundered in the midst of a series of upheavals, watched a popular television show about a white, "blended" family called the Brady Bunch with longing, and was certain that everyone else's family was more coherent and stable, more "family-like," than my own. I tested my hypothesis by spending an inordinate amount of time at the homes of my friends, convinced I could find the missing ingredient, the rarefied glue that coalesced seemingly random individuals into indivisible clans.

When I was ten, I stayed nights in a tiny apartment with a friend whose mother slept the entire time I visited—the only hours she didn't have to work. In seventh grade, I spent weekends with my best friend amidst shaky, broken-down stairs, entire walls of peeling paint, and an angry father who punished his children for the tiniest indiscretion. At thirteen, I was a regular fixture at the house of a friend whose dad smoked what was known in the neighborhood as "the best fucking pot in the state." We chanted along to "We don't need no education" in his cave-like study, oblivious to the irony that he was a teacher at the high school his daughter and I would eventually attend.

I also visited families that didn't skirt the edge of acceptable middle class–dom. I met, for instance, a lovely family on a bus tour of Ireland. Everyone in the family had names starting with the letter S, and they invited me to stay at their midcentury modern house in upstate New York. I found it a little dull, but charming nonetheless. I felt the same way about a nice, middle-class family—the father was a doctor, the mother a schoolteacher—living next door. Their young daughter and I shoveled spoonfuls of coveted (but verboten at my house) Marshmallow Fluff into our mouths, and romped through each floor of her Marimekko'd house with abandon.

By the time I graduated from high school, I had concluded that some families were like mine—they broke the rules and made up new ones as they went along, with hit-or-miss results. And some families were not like mine—they hewed to a more traditional path that appeared more stable, but lacked the frisson of experimentation. The first group explored new territory, but couldn't determine a workable cartography for the future. The latter followed a decades-old map, dangerously oblivious to tectonic shifts occurring beneath the surface.

By the time I had my son fifteen years later, I had made several attempts to create a family of my own. I winged it, searching for stability but stumbling over patterns of intimacy that seemed built into my DNA. There was a relationship with a sexy musician who may or may not have been on drugs. There was a guy who lived six thousand miles and twenty cultural galaxies away. My high school sweetheart followed me across the country for my first two years of college, but my working night and day on a documentary one hot summer in a borrowed condo on the Upper East Side of Manhattan ripped our relationship to shreds. Then I fell for a guy who was kind of right for me. But he came from an intact family and his parents had pictures of him and his sisters all over the walls of the house they'd lived in for twenty-five years, and every time I slept over (in a separate bedroom, of course), I felt like an insecure freak from a broken home. Which eventually made him crazy and swear, to my face, that he would never again go out with anyone whose parents were divorced.

It was a lot of fun.

So when my son was born and I saw him lying strapped to a board under an oxygen tent, unable to breathe on his own because he'd had a difficult birth with all sorts of complications, I realized I had to get my proverbial stuff together. Decisions had to be made. Promises had to be kept. I couldn't just shake my head and say I tried my best if he told me one day I had been an awful mother and he wanted—no, needed—to live in the desert in a tent with his pet iguana. I listened to his raspy breathing and let the reality of responsibility wash over me. It was now or never, I thought to myself. Romantic love doth not a family make. Bogus, manufactured ideas of following your bliss can lead you over a cliff without a parachute. Make some sane, considered decisions and live with them for a while. If they don't work, reevaluate and change the plan. Make sure the boy doesn't suffer unnecessarily in the process. Take responsibility. Grow up.

Which was also a lot of fun, and, given my track record, as likely as gathering odds and ends from my kitchen, building a rocket ship, and flying to the moon. To my credit, though, by the time I went into labor, I had learned a few things. I knew I wasn't willing to follow any doctrine, including "attachment parenting," blindly. I was certain I didn't want to "just do what felt right in the moment" again, either. I knew I had to create a hybrid modality, a stable but adaptive platform for family life. Like the operating system on my computer, it had to be sophisticated enough to handle several programs at once without crashing, or worse, blowing the motherboard.

I decided to put the family-watching skills I developed as a child to use by editing a collection of essays about contemporary families that balance the traditional and the countercultural, the cliché and the experimental. I jumped into the project because I wasn't alone in my search to be both authentic and sane. My friends and colleagues had also recovered from childhoods full of too much or too little, and were looking to fashion an adulthood out of wisdom gained. Hours and hours of their lives were devoted to researching and integrating elements that could make their crazy, complex twenty-first-century families work. My book would be the ultimate reference book for all of us, I thought, a modern anthology version of Dr. Spock.

When I started to talk about the project with friends, I was taken aback by the stories that poured in. A man had stopped working and embraced poverty to be at home with his kids and thought all men should do the same. A couple lived in a cohousing community—part commune and part superluxe modern prefab. Another woman had married her dog, and found the relationship infinitely more satisfying than the one she had with her ex-husband. A bisexual couple spent half the year with each other, and the other six months with their other, opposite-gendered lovers. An activist from Boston organized on behalf of the legal recognition of friendships.

I was shocked by how many people were searching for

authenticity through experimentation. The configurations seemed endless, but to me, the child of one such earlier experiment, the challenges did too. Before long I was back in junior high, peering into my friends' living rooms and looking for answers. Only this time, I was looking for stability, complexity, longevity, and overall satisfaction. When I saw those four elements in a family, no matter what it looked like, I paid closer attention. I wanted to know more. I commissioned an essay.

Two years later, I am happy to report that I have learned something about how to be a family from each and every writer in this book, and collectively their insights comprise the best list of guidelines for the twenty-first-century family a person could ever want. Talking about her open marriage, Jenny Block says we have to make every decision that affects our families with extreme care, putting the needs of everyone in the family at the forefront. In her essay about becoming a single mother, asha bandele says hopes and dreams can only go so far—emotional needs must be met in order for a family to thrive. On marrying her gay best friend to keep him in the country, Liza Monroy says that even the law cannot obstruct actions we sometimes must take on behalf of the ones we love.

On the surface, Sasha Hom's modern nomadic family seems almost too fluid, but dig a little deeper and it's clear the Hom family makes decisions with staggering commitment and the intention to persevere—two components I now deem necessary for family life. Neal Pollack and husband-and-wife team Marc and Amy Vachon solve the problem of part-time househusbandry in very different ways, but the core family principle couldn't be any clearer: split the workload. Suzanne Kamata and Susan McKinney de Ortega, who live in Japan and Mexico, respectively, with their husbands, say that intercultural families can work beautifully, but agree that differences cannot be glossed over, and surrendering at least some of your expectations is essential.

Min Jin Lee and ZZ Packer say it's rarely bad to challenge assumptions about race, class, and social circumstance, but suggest we do it responsibly—without disrupting the applecart so much that we injure ourselves, or our kids. Paula Penn-Nabrit and Dawn Friedman say that whether exhausting, or heartbreaking, the decisions we make should benefit our families not just today or tomorrow, but two, three, or even six decades from now. Amy Anderson says a family can never be too big, too small, or too blended. Judith Levine says money can't buy love, but it does play an important role in every relationship and should be examined accordingly.

One of the most affirming aspects of working on this book has been learning of the extraordinary decisions writers have made on behalf of their families. Dan Savage adopts a son, keeps the door open for his son's drug-addicted mom, and lets his ordinary defenses give way to something larger than fear and judgment. Antonio Caya gives his DNA to a woman who longs for a child, and follows something infinitely more intelligent than his intellect. Meredith Maran implores a friend to reconsider filing for divorce, revisits the trauma of her own divorce, and summons compassion not just for her friend, but for herself.

In the final essay of the book, Rebecca Barry buys a ramshackle fantasy house, puts her foot through the floor, and ends up in couples therapy with her sister.

All in the name of making one big happy family.

There is so much to be learned here, but I welcome you to this book with the big idea that a great family, like a great piece of art, is made one decision at a time. Each essay proves we create our families with the choices we make every day. No family is a cakewalk, but if we abandon dogma and arrogance, tradition and happenstance, we are left with information and faith. Our only option is to think deeply about every step, move forward with discipline and an eye toward longevity and the greater good, and have faith we have done the right thing. If ten years pass and our family is thriving, we know we've made good decisions. If ten years pass and it's falling apart, well, we can credit our decisions for that too.

My son is almost four years old. Our house has good days and bad days, but overall, life is sane, stable, and happy. I am no longer winging it. I don't look to other families for the answer. Some decisions are more difficult to make than others, but my partner and I, sometimes kicking and screaming, try to make the best ones possible.

So far, it's made all the difference.

One Big Happy Family

1.
And Then We Were Poly Jenny Block

I was seventeen when my sexual education began.

"You are responsible for your own orgasm," my boyfriend told me. He was the guy I lost my virginity to, the guy I had my first orgasm with, and the guy whose words would one day become my mantra: I am responsible for my own orgasm. I believe that literally and figuratively. In bed, I play an active role in getting what I want. But I also take charge of getting what I want throughout my sexual life. That's why, along with a husband I adore, I have lovers. My husband, Christopher, and I have an open marriage, a polyamorous marriage, in fact. I know it may sound decadent, or like a throwback to the "free love" of the sixties. But really, for all the hype, "open marriage" is just one of many ways to negotiate love and sex and marriage. We haven't been doing it that long, but it now seems so obvious. Like, "Why on earth didn't we think of this before?"

I have always liked sex. I mean really, really liked sex. I have been accused, in fact, of "thinking like a man." That is, of seeing sex as something wholly separate from love. When my husband and I first started dating, it was obvious even then that our drives were quite different. As much as he enjoyed sex, he didn't need or want it as often as I did. But I fell so madly in love with him, I figured it didn't matter.

I was terribly wrong.

Three years into our marriage, I began to feel itchy. So I had an affair. She was beautiful, an artist I met through a mutual friend. I deliberately chose to have an affair with a woman, rationalizing that it wasn't as bad as sleeping with another man. (Simply by virtue of his gender, my husband could never be for me what she could be.)

She wasn't the first woman I'd been with. When Christopher and I began dating, I told him that I was bisexual. "I don't care who you were with before," he told me. "But once it's just you and me, it's just you and me." And that's why—as lovely and sweet as my affair with Artist Girl was—it was awful too. I felt sick about lying to my husband, sick about wanting to be with her, sick for not just calling it off—or avoiding it in the first place.

I thought hard about how I had gotten there. At first, I figured that my being with her really was about my bisexuality, about a part of me that I simply couldn't brush aside.

But the more I thought about it, the more I realized that wasn't true: it was about wanting more sex than my husband could offer, and sex different from that which any one person could provide.

My relationship with Artist Girl ended very, very badly. One night while in bed with her husband, she told him about us, foolishly thinking it would "turn him on." It didn't. He

was furious and threatened to tell my husband. I knew I had
to tell him myself. When I confessed, he was crushed, more
because I had lied to him than because I had slept with her.
I cried and cried, wondering if I had destroyed my marriage,
if he would leave me, but also wondering if I would ever be
happy, ever be sexually satisfied, ever find a way to make this
work.

We didn't talk about it much for several years. He couldn't.
I would ask him once in a while if he was okay, and he would
tell me he was fine. Eventually, I believed him. I kept my nose
clean, and we were bumping along—hitting rough patches,
but bumping along. We had an adequate sex life; probably
pretty darn good by some standards. Still, there were always
things I wanted that I simply couldn't get from him.

"I want you to talk dirty to me," I told him. "To tie me up.
To attack me in the middle of the day on the kitchen floor."

"I can't, baby," he'd say, drawing me into his arms. "I love
you."

And slowly I began to figure it out. For Christopher, sex with
me was about loving me.

And loving me was about caring for and respecting me.
Although there are people who can manage that duality (or
plurality), my husband simply couldn't. And I wasn't sure he
should have to. But I also wasn't sure that I should have to go
without.

One day, on a whim, really, I asked Christopher about a
longtime friend of mine. She had once been a grad student at
the university where I taught. I had helped her get through

research papers, exams, and first-time teaching assignments. She spent a lot of long nights and weekend afternoons at our house during those two years, and we became close friends. Even after finishing her degree, she still spent a lot of time at the house.

"Have you ever thought about sleeping with her?" I asked him.

"No," he said. My husband has no poker face. "Okay, yes, but . . ."

"But what?" I asked.

"Well, first of all, she'd never want to sleep with me. She's ten years younger than I am."

"Actually, she's dying to sleep with you. She tells me all the time."

My husband made a face, wrinkling up his nose and shaking his head at me in disbelief. Then he paused and said, "Besides, I don't want to be with anyone else."

"Really?" I asked.

"Well," he said, "I mean, I don't need to."

"But do you want to?" I didn't need him to answer me. It was clear that, in his head, he was already there.

"She's hot," he said.

"I know." I laughed. "So . . . ?"

"So, of course I'd like to sleep with her. But what about you?"

"Of course," I replied. "I'd like to sleep with her too, silly."

"That's not what I meant," he said.

"I know. I know. So . . . ?"

"So, bring it on," he teased.

It was true—I knew she was interested. We'd joked about it plenty of times before.

"When are you going to let me at that hot husband of yours?" she'd ask me.

"Whenever you like," I'd tell her. I started teasing Christopher about it every now and then. Sometimes when we'd have sex I'd talk about her being there. It always pushed him over the edge.

Finally, I decided it was time.

"Let's do it," I said to her one night when we were at my house, watching yet another terrible made-for-TV movie. She knew exactly what I was talking about.

"You sure?" she asked.

"Are you?" I asked back.

"Yeah," she said. "As long as you're positive it won't mess us up."

"I don't think it will," I said. "But you know I can't promise that."

"I know," she said. "But promise me, anyway."

"Okay," I told her. "I promise."

A few hours later, Christopher came home. He slid onto the couch next to me, putting his hand on my right thigh, under the throw blanket. Her hand was already on my left. A few seconds later, I felt their hands accidentally touch, and I saw them look at each other. I'm pretty sure that was the exact moment Christopher realized what was going on.

. . .

"I'm beat," he said a short while later. "I'm going to bed."

"We'll be up soon," I said. He kissed me and began to walk away.

"What about me?" she asked. He looked at me, and then kissed her, long and hard.

Laughing, he shook his head.

"You girls," he said, as he headed upstairs. When the movie ended, we followed. We slipped into bed with Christopher as if we'd done it a hundred times before, one on either side of him.

Everything that followed felt equally natural.

It was amazing to watch them together. It was hot, but it was also very sweet. She was so lost in him, and he in her. I was able to see him as a human being, if you know what I mean. Not as my husband or my daughter's father, but as a man, a sexual being, a person who wants to be wanted, who needs to be wanted.

And I know that watching her and me together was an incredible experience for him as well. She even taught him how to give me a G-spot orgasm, a feat that he had never managed. It sounds so deviant, I know. But it was charming, really. He held her long hair in his hands and watched her. He also stole looks at me. "I love you," he mouthed. "I love you, too," I somehow managed. And when I came, I couldn't help but notice the glances the two of them exchanged. "Not bad," his seemed to say. "See, I could teach you a thing or two," hers seemed to imply. It was weird. But it was also, well, normal.

My husband and I had a six-month affair with my close friend. The three of us had sex. He and she had sex. She and I had sex. And, of course, he and I continued to have sex, just the two of us. The arrangement eventually faded out, and we all slipped back into our previous relationships. But my marriage was forever changed. Our experience with her was the catalyst that led us to explore open marriage and, ultimately, polyamory.

It's been interesting and hard and wonderful and confusing. It has led to some terribly sad moments and some incredibly joyful ones. The sad ones always stem from some combination of ego, insecurity, and lack of communication. The wonderful ones result from love and trust and understanding. But really, it's blindingly simple. We give each other what we need, including freedom and space. We respect each other. And we are self-aware enough to know that we're interested in, and capable of, exploring sex, whatever that means for us and despite what it may mean for anyone else. (That is, of course, anyone not sexually involved with us.) It has brought Christopher and me closer than I ever imagined possible.

We communicate in ways I never dreamed of, staying up late at night talking about the nature of monogamy, of sexuality, of marriage, and of life in general. I suppose open marriage works for us for precisely that reason: because we talk about it, because it has opened us to each other. The learning curve certainly has been steep. We have absolutely, positively no models for what we're doing. We're really just the average couple next door. Really. We've just found that "owning" each other sexually doesn't help our marriage.

It only hurts it.

It is amazing, though, how much trouble people have with open marriage. One person told me how sad he is that I need "conquests" and need others to find me sexually attractive to be satisfied, and that he hopes that one day I'll find enough success elsewhere to overcome that. Another person told me she thinks I'm a lesbian who doesn't want to give up the creature comforts my marriage provides. Still another said she's scared for me and my relationship if I need such "fireworks." But each of these statements said more about the speaker than about me.

The truth is, I'm just like everyone else. I'm just trying to figure out all of this life stuff. It's hard. There's this one plan we're all supposed to follow, this heterosexual, monogamous, child-rearing, one-size-fits-all model that we're all supposed to goose-step into line with. But I can't. In fact, I have a responsibility not to. I am responsible for my own orgasm—and my own happiness. And I don't need other people to like me or to approve, and I don't need others to live in the same way I do. I just need to do what I need to do, without hurting myself or others. And at this point in my marriage, at least, that means having sexual relationships outside of my marriage.

Christopher hasn't pursued anyone since my friend. He says he's too shy to pick up girls, and, really, he doesn't feel the need. I can sometimes tell that the fact that I do hurts him.

"Intellectually," he explains, "I totally get it. But sometimes, emotionally, it's hard."

"I know," I tell him. "Do you need me to stop?"

"No," he says. "I'm not that guy. But you have to bear with me. I'm still trying to figure all of this out."

"Hey," I reply. "Me too."

And it's true. Neither of us really knows how we feel or what will or won't work until we test it out. For example, Christopher wrestled for a time with how much he does and does not want to know. When I was with another woman, he wanted every gory detail. But when I was with another man, all he wanted to know was who and when. If he asks for specific information, I answer. Sometimes, however, it is hard to read whether he really wants that answer, and I feel sad when I get it wrong. Like when I don't tell him something and it comes up later, making him feel out of the loop, something I try desperately to avoid. It all boils down to effective communication—without it, no marriage, open or otherwise, stands a chance.

Being secretive, lying, or sneaking around—those would be surefire ways to destroy our marriage. But the sex itself is not a threat. I think of it as the "playpen effect": you keep a kid locked up in one of those things and all she thinks about is how to get out, how much she'll love what's in the other room. But let her roam free and check it all out, and odds are she'll end up at your feet, playing with a puzzle. Is there a chance she'll love another room and stay in there instead? Sure. Just like there's always a chance one of us will fall in love with someone else and decide to end our marriage. But I don't think that having sex outside our marriage increases that risk. In fact, I believe it decreases it, because it removes all the fantasy. I don't pine. If I want someone (and he or she wants me), then I have him or her. So far, no one has come even close to making me want to jump ship. But I'll tell you the truth: before we tried out this open marriage thing, I definitely wondered about the quality of the grass in other lawns.

Making this work has been much less dramatic than one might imagine. Sex is a happy thing, a good thing. If I can find happiness in something so simple, without hurting anyone, why wouldn't I? There's no one swinging from our chandeliers. We don't attend parties with fishbowls for keys at the door. And our daughter isn't exposed to any sort of debauched behavior. None of this affects her at all, in fact, because she never sees anything out of the ordinary. When my friend stayed over, she was always back in the guest room before our daughter woke up, and she slept over as much before and after the affair as during. And there have been no other lovers in our home. Putting our needs before our daughter's well-being is never an option.

My pattern of lovers fluctuated for a few years. There were times when I had a steady or two, men I kept in touch with after our initial "meeting." There was my Skier Philosopher, who sent me delicious e-mails and met me for marathon nights in lavish hotels; my Playboy Analyst, who was the best friend of the guy my best friend was dating and who was happy to "take me in" when I visited her; my Young Romantic, who called me now and again, and would make plans to see me when he was in town. But mostly there were more anonymous trysts. That just seemed to be where I was at the time. Men—or women—I met when I was out of town, spent a night or two with, and then never saw or talked to again. You know, it seems to me that lots of people are basically in open marriages: they have illicit affairs. Christopher and I simply decided we were ready to be honest, with ourselves and with each other, about what we want and need.

This is in no way a prescription for anyone else. All I know is how I feel, which is loved and cherished and secure—thanks to my husband. I want that. But I don't see anything wrong with wanting more. And, for me, that "more" is longing. Mystery. Sexual tension. Craving—and getting tastes of—things I never wholly possess.

Why am I married, then? Many people have asked me that question. So I'll tell you exactly what I tell them. As hot as it makes me when a new conquest whispers something scandalous in my ear, nothing thrills me like the sound of Christopher's voice when I hear him say, "Hey, baby, I'm home."

Now, this is the part in the film where the text "Three Years Later" flashes across the screen because, you see, it was after those three years that things shifted for us.

"I want you to kiss me," she said. Funny she should use those words when they so closely echoed mine more than ten years before. "I want to kiss you," I had said to my then best friend, Sophie Anne. "Me too," Sophie Anne had said to me then. "Are you sure?" was what I said to Jemma, the girl who was now requesting that I do something that I imagined could change a lot of things for a lot of people. Of course, I never could have known then just how much change it would mean.

I met Jemma at an art gallery. She was curating a show that I was reviewing for the paper. "Can I help you?" she asked. I was standing in front of a massive canvas, taking notes as I took in the colors, textures, and designs. I introduced myself and told her why I was there. "Let me get you a catalog," she said. When she came back she invited me to the official opening and lecture that night. That was the first of many outings we would go on together. As friends, of course.

She had told me she was straight. "Very straight. I don't have a problem with it. I just can't imagine ever being with a girl," she said when I told her one day that I identified as bisexual. Between that and the fact that she was eleven years my junior, a work contact, and not my type, I never gave a moment's thought to us ever being more than friends. But after about six months of spending time together, we went away on a weekend trip. I do some travel writing and sometimes can take someone along. It was on that trip that she asked me to kiss her.

"Where is this coming from?" I asked. I couldn't have been more surprised if she had asked me to rob a bank with her. Here was this straitlaced, adorable, intelligent young blonde asking me to kiss her. Part of my shock stemmed from the fact that we spent so much of our time together talking about everything, especially about sex and love and relationships. She had been through some rough stuff in that department and had come to me to talk about much of it. So you would have thought I would have had at least an inkling. But I was as blindsided as a girl could be. Honest to goodness.

"I don't know. I just know I want you to kiss me," she said. And I did. That was one year and seven months ago and she has been my girlfriend ever since. I'm still married, of course, and adore my husband, Christopher, as much as ever. But since that very first kiss, I not only haven't had any other lovers, I haven't wanted any. After my husband and I opened our marriage about five years ago, I had a handful of other lovers. It was fun. And it was exciting. But it was never love. After just a short time with Jemma, I knew it was something different.

I have gotten in the habit of calling my relationship with my husband an open marriage, strictly for lack of a better term. But it wasn't until I met Jemma that I started calling it polyamorous for one very simple reason: I love her. When I started seeing her, my heart expanded just like when someone has a second child. As much as the expectant parents might worry that couldn't be possible, it is. There is no shortage of love to go around when there are people around to love. What a great word, *polyamory*. Many loves. Who wouldn't want that? Of course, I could hardly believe it was possible myself until I was in it. Wouldn't I fall out of love with my husband? Wouldn't it be a scheduling disaster? What will my kid think? Aren't I just immoral or a slut or a freak?

But the truth is, I love Christopher as much now as ever. Nothing, not even scheduling, is a burden when it comes to love. Emily, my daughter, thinks Jemma is my best friend, nothing more and nothing less. And she is my best friend. Emily knows I love Jemma, and, in fact, Emily loves her too. But I don't tell Emily about my interest in porn or my toy collection or anything else about my sex life. So why would this be any different? It's the only part of my relationship with Jemma that I keep from her, for now, and rightly so. She hasn't asked about sex and suddenly providing this information without a foundation seems inappropriate and out of context.

As far as when we will tell Emily more, well, in a way, that's up to her. I suppose it might seem strange in some way that because of the nature of my work as a writer, the general public will know the whole of my relationship with Jemma before Emily will. But that goes for a number of things in my life. The essay about my having plastic surgery came out before Emily was old enough to talk to about it, and I still haven't told her about the sex-toy party I hosted and wrote about, nor have I told her about how impossible I found it to care for my mother when she was fighting breast cancer. Kids can't know everything about their parents, and that poses a double whammy for writers' kids. But it does not in any way imply that I feel bad about the choices I have made.

In terms of what we will tell her, that's a no-brainer—what we'll tell her is the truth. People live and love differently, and Mommy and Daddy don't think that marriage precludes loving other people and that includes having sexual relationships with other people. I will answer my daughter's questions openly and age-appropriately. If that comes sooner rather than later because of my work, that is, if someone says to her, "My mommy says that your mommy has a girlfriend," then so be it. You know, my father is a rabbi and that came with all sorts of not-fun stuff in terms of being a rabbi's kid. And you know what my father would say, "Those 'em the breaks, kid."

At the time I just thought he was being a big meanie. But he was right. And the same thing goes for Emily. I'm sure there will be times when she wishes I wrote about kittens instead of love and sex or that my work entailed baking cupcakes instead of revealing my life. But I also hope there will be even more times when she is proud of the work I do and understand why I handled things as I did. Some parents travel all the time. Some parents work for companies that the general public despises. And some of us write about our lives. It's hard for me to imagine at this age that someone is going to say something directly to her. And, who knows, at the time of this printing, I may have already spilled the beans. But that will be about her readiness and nothing more.

My husband adores Jemma as well. She often comes over for dinner or spends the weekend at our place, playing Scrabble with me, watching *Hannah Montana* with Emily, or talking wine and recipes with Christopher. That's the extent of Christopher and Jemma's relationship. It's purely platonic. As of this writing, Christopher doesn't have any outside lovers. His choice, of course. Turns out there are plenty of couples out there in the same boat, where one partner chooses to exercise his or her freedom to have outside partners and the other does not. The truth is, equity in a relationship stems from having freedom, not necessarily from acting upon it, and Christopher's choice, he'll be the first to tell you, does not mean in any way that he is unhappy with mine.

And as for being immoral, a slut, or a freak, well, those are judgments, and I like to remember that old saying about glass houses. Besides, I discovered there are a whole lot of people out there in open and swinging and poly and other "alternative" lifestyles. And the ones I know, anyway, have proven to be thoughtful, kind, intelligent people who are trying to figure out their way in the world, just like anyone else. And if name-calling is required, which I wish we could skip altogether, there are just as many immoral people and sluts and freaks in the monogamous world as there are in the polyamorous one. And monogamous relationships fail just as polyamorous ones do. How many people you have sex with or love doesn't speak to your character, just to your choices.

Sound boring? It is. Wonderfully, perfectly, normally boring. I don't regret for a second the way things were before Jemma, and I would never be so presumptuous as to suggest I know the paths my life might take in the future. But that's just it. Life is a journey. And as far as my sexuality goes, that journey has included so many things, from monogamy to open marriage to polyamory and from heterosexuality to bisexuality. It's all a spectrum, as far as I can tell—gender, sexuality, relationships, love. We all fit somewhere on it with very few of us at either end. It isn't always easy to choose that gray area in between. But, for me, it has always been worth it.

2.
Woman Up **asha bandele**

It's 1995, September 30, and my husband and I are about to have a honeymoon of sorts. It'll be a forty-eight-hour—or, to be exact, forty-four-hour—jaunt in a trailer at the New York State prison compound where Rashid lives. He's lived in one or another of the nearly hundred prisons that have come to define the landscape of upstate New York since 1983, when he was convicted of a gang-related murder at eighteen. I'd met him in 1990, when I was a twenty-three-year-old college student teaching and reading poetry to women and men who were incarcerated. I believed then, as I do now, that poems can enlarge a heart, expand a soul. They had done so for me and I was watching them do it for prisoners and especially for Rashid, who, when we met, was already a voracious reader, already a man seeking transformation.

Slowly, over about a year, and over discussions about changing ourselves and our world, we fell in love, Rashid and I, and eventually, when I could no longer stand not being able to touch this man who, through his insights and warmth and dreams, had so touched me, we married, there, at the prison. An interminable five months after we exchanged vows in a visiting room, we qualified for conjugal visits—"trailers" in jailhouse vernacular. The prison issued us a date, and in a small two-bedroom trailer in a yard on the prison compound we made love, again and again. No place was off-limits. We made love in the bathroom, on the sheets I bought just for the occasion, in the bedroom, in the kitchenette while I was trying to make coffee. But more than that, so much more, we had a period of seminormalcy. We made curried chicken and roti together, danced slow to Al Green, watched the news, showered together. For five years, for forty-four hours every three to five months, this was our life, the life we chose.

Even all these years later I remember that first time as though we'd recorded it, as though I'd watched a videotape every night thereafter, meticulously memorizing each movement, each pause, each laugh, all the things we said, all the things we did not say. I remember how I hadn't said to him then, that first time, that I would never have a baby with him while he was locked up. I knew many, many other women with incarcerated husbands chose to do so, and while I did not disparage their decisions, I knew it wasn't for me. I could not see being a single parent. I certainly could not imagine bringing a baby into a prison. I may have made that choice for myself, but I was an adult, willingly taking on the emotional slop that loving a person who's imprisoned can create. A child was an innocent, unable to weigh all sides of the equation. I could not do that to a baby.

But in September 1995, I hadn't made such grand pronouncements to Rashid because I didn't believe then that I could get pregnant. I'd had so much sex in my life, had twice lived with men, had been married once before, and had never gotten pregnant. I went up to the facility and made love with and to my husband and I did not worry. Three weeks later, I discovered I was pregnant.

I never considered keeping the baby. Even as I wept, rubbed my abdomen, claimed my child, listened to Rashid's pleading that I not have an abortion, I never once considered it. How could I? It wasn't just the prison or my unwillingness to be a single parent. It was also financial. I wasn't working. I was living in a room in someone else's home, barely eking out an income as a writer and poet. I had just returned to school—finally, after more than a decade—to finish my bachelor's degree. What did I have to offer a child, save for anxiety and instability? Rashid and I argued bitterly—something we'd never really done before—about the decision, but all he could offer me were religious platitudes about life being sacred. What about mine? I'd argue back. Is my life sacred too? I didn't need commandments, I said to my husband. I needed cash. I needed physical support.

Against my husband's wishes, and against the love I felt for that baby who had barely begun to take shape inside of me, on a cold Thursday in November 1995, I had an abortion. In a clinic that was less a medical facility than a factory, I sat in a hard plastic chair with rows and rows of other women, some far younger than I, some shockingly older. When my name was finally called and I had dispensed with the routine tests—blood work and such—I was led into the ice-cold room where the procedure would take place. Despite the two doctors and the two nurses who were there, and all those women waiting just outside for their turn on the table, it may have been the most alone I've ever felt in my life. I collapsed into hysteria, crying so hard that the anesthesiologist worried my breathing would be impaired. When I thought about it later, I realized that I probably should have been sent home that day, told to think my decision through more. That didn't happen, and fifteen minutes later I woke up in the recovery area no longer pregnant.

Despite my resolve, my choice to have an abortion—something I knew was absolutely the right thing to do at that time in my life—I carried guilt about it for years. Terminating my pregnancy—I felt this then and I feel it now—was against the natural order of things. Had Rashid *not* been in prison and had we been married under normal circumstances, I surely would have had my baby. Or, if our life *sans* prison presented itself in such a way that financially or otherwise we could not bring the baby to term, I would have done much greater soul-searching before making my decision. The choice would not have seemed so obvious. But I knew, lying on that examination table in November 1995, that no matter what difficulty, I could not go through an abortion with my husband again. The weight of destroying something that was created from a place of great love was unbearable. I carried it once. To do it a second time would, literally, crush me. I told Rashid that. In those raw, ragged days following the procedure, I promised Rashid that if I ever, ever became pregnant again, even if he was still in prison, I would have the baby. Four years later, in 1999, I would have to stand by those words.

In July of that year I was somewhere in the midst of a book tour when Rashid and I were issued a date for a trailer visit. I flew home from California, packed everything we would need—food, sheets, towels, juice, birth control. It was less than a week before my period was supposed to come. I had no fears or even thoughts about pregnancy. I was thinking about my career, what was next on the literary horizon. Rashid and I talked about my dreams, his dreams, and we made love and celebrated the book and made love some more. A week later, when my period was a couple of days late, it didn't even occur to me that I might be pregnant. But after six or seven days had gone by, I decided, reluctantly, to buy a test. Fast as I could pee on a stick, the thing was developing dark pink double lines that could not be misread or denied. When Rashid called the next day I told him directly. We're having a baby, I said.

Unlike with our first pregnancy, I never thought *not* to have this baby. First of all, that she could create herself in spite of spermicides and a low-ovulation moment indicated to me that her presence was beyond any choice I had to make. And then, too, I was getting older; I was thirty-two when Nisa was conceived. Perhaps I would not have another chance to be the one thing I knew I always wanted to be: a mother. Still, there were fears.

Some were evident. I was an author and freelance writer when I became pregnant. Would I find a real job and decent child care? Could I survive the predicted sleep deprivation alone? For that matter, would I be able to go through labor without my husband? And though I know it's ultimately self-defeating, I worried about what people would think. As the child of parents who had been married forty-four years when I became pregnant, what did I look like, appearing as I did, a single mother? And okay, yes, being a Black woman factored into the image piece: I mean, did I look like some statistic walking around pregnant with no man in sight? The idea of that was, for me, intolerable.

I have, for as long as I've been conscious of it, refused to wear the jacket some racist sewed for me. But in what real way could I fight back? My attempts were, at best, pathetic: painfully, with the aid of lotion, water, and soap, I squeezed my wedding rings onto my fingers long after they'd swollen into things that looked more like fat little sausages. In doctors' offices and later at the midwifery center where I gave birth, I looked at no one, sat up proudly, and made calls on my cell phone to girlfriends, figuring Rashid, or "my husband," as I proclaimed a little too loudly, into the conversation. When the time came, I paid for private birthing classes so I would not have to sit with other women as their loving partners caressed their bellies.

But I worried most of all about protection. Would I be able to raise a Black girl safely in a world that seems only to expand in its ability to hate and destroy? In a culture tipped toward death, with Black people and women more often than not the stand-ins for the bull's-eye, would the life of one Black girl be honored by anyone other than me? Would my love and honor be enough to sustain her through to maturity? The constantly rising rates of drug and alcohol abuse among young people; the sexual and physical violence that have become integrated into pop culture as though it's a sexy goddamn courting ritual; the girls who at eight years old are giving blow jobs in the schoolhouse stairwells; and the groundswell of so-called good girls out on the stroll in

Brooklyn, Atlanta, *and* the suburbs, simply put, scared the shit out of me.

Not because I judged or disliked any of these kids, but because I'd been my own eighties version of them. I knew how that slippery slope could be a challenge to circumvent. Would my little girl be able to do what I wasn't? My own childhood was enchanted in many ways that both count and don't count. Against a Manhattan backdrop, my sister and I were given music and dance lessons, horseback riding, swimming, and art classes. I attended fine private schools, the ballet. I saw Judith Jamison dance *Cry.* But it was also a childhood punctured by loneliness and violence. What my parents could give me in terms of education and culture was no armor against the excesses and dangers of high school, of growing up in an urban environment too large, too unwieldy to notice its children coming undone. Worse for me—I see this now, though not then—I was so very young. I began high school at twelve, graduated at fifteen, and while I could put on the makeup and heels and stumble behind girls older than I was, I could not in any way negotiate the social settings—bars and clubs we lied to our parents about and faked our way into. There were date rapes by men much older than I was. There were other assaults, psychological and physical. There was always racism. *Piss-colored nigger-Rican* is the term I remember best.

When my child reached an age when she too would have to negotiate streets and sex and perhaps even simple fucking survival, would she know how to speak to me, as I did not know how to speak to my parents? Would I know how to listen to her, hear what she was telling me, read between her lines? My parents, in all of their brilliance and commitment, were unable to do that for me. During my childhood, puberty, and later, teenage angst became the nomenclature for what eventually revealed itself as a clinical depression that at its height spiraled into suicidal ideation. It would be years, so many, before I could name the hurt, try to heal it. Would I repeat a vile pattern with my daughter? After all, I had both of my parents present, loving me. My daughter only had me. These questions, more than the physical challenges of pregnancy, kept me awake through the nights, staring at everything and nothing and wondering, worrying, where could I go, where could I live and raise my child safely? In 2000, the year my daughter was born, the only thing the nightly news was reporting was the presidential campaign, rooted in the reclamation of family values, and headed by a man who signed 153 death warrants during his turn as governor. I wanted to run, go live off the grid, have my child, tell no one, keep her forever in my womb.

Of course disappearance was not an option, though I thought of it at regular intervals. I had to stay connected to Rashid, even as excursions into the prison became more and more hellish, our love no longer the matrix disguising the blight, the stench. A question, a terrible question took form in my head, my heart. Would I still, as a mother, be able to navigate the prisons and my relationship with Nisa's father, the person who was closest to me in the world?

But the rounder my tummy became, the more my breasts

swelled, the more these fears either fell away or shrank into something I could manage. I gave myself over to reason, faith, hope, Dr. Spock. I did find work, and finally, after starts and stops, I found incredible child care too. And I did make it through labor—according to many, quite easily. Although Nisa came two weeks late, when my water did break at exactly 12:01 a.m. on April 14, 2000, she came quickly. Less than eleven hours after labor began, my daughter was in my arms, having already learned to latch on. Seven hours after that, we were home entertaining people, eating gourmet take-out pizza.

Sometimes my sister or a close friend will say what a good mother I am but, they will add, they don't know how I do it, how I even made the decision to become a single mother. This was a comment I heard especially during the first two years of Nisa's life, when I was writing a novel and working full-time *and* meeting my deadlines. Yes, I said when asked, it was hard, impossibly hard. I hated—I still hate—having to be the sole emotional and financial provider. The pressure's too great, I said once to my sister. The idea that if you slip, no one will be there to catch you, but worse, no one will be there to catch your baby. It's a responsibility you can neither fully handle nor ever shirk. So, yes, yes, I say, somewhere between potty training, playdates, speaking engagements, bylines, and balancing the household books I lost pieces of myself I am only now trying to reclaim. I started smoking cigarettes again, spent too many nights on my couch after I got my daughter to sleep, drinking wine and crying. The depression of my teenage years returned.

Yes, I told my sister, one night when I was halfway though a bottle of wine, there are times I'm sure I've lost my mind completely. And no, I told her, no, I could not hold my marriage together.

Caring for Rashid and Nisa at the same time was far more than I could bear—the weekly treks through metal detectors and bars, the parts of your spirit that always seem to get snagged by the ever-present razor wire. I take Nisa to see her father, but for me to be romantically entangled with him now, when as a parent I need him most but most feel his absence, is just too painful. When it was me alone, the denial and deprivation that necessarily accompany a prison marriage were bad enough. With my daughter now in the equation it means that every second I see her grow, change, fall down, stand up again is a second I am reminded that the only other person who loves her as I do is not there to be a witness.

I thought Rashid's absence when I became a mother would be all about needing someone to help carry the groceries into the house or cover the utility bills. But the worst part of it all, the part that chokes in my throat, is that I have no one with whom to share the everyday beauty and wonder of my child. No one who will ever lose an hour of time, as I still regularly do, just watching her sleep. How could I live with that? How could I live with the fact that my husband embodied the idea that there was both someone and no one to witness her with me, raise a hand and testify, speak in tongues about the most beautiful thing we could ever have, ever hope to have? I couldn't play at house or marriage anymore. I think that's what I said to Rashid finally. I needed the real thing, or I needed to woman up and do this on my own.

That breakup, though it left me with a grief so profound it has no name I can call, is something that feels akin to losing my husband, best friend, father, and brother on the very same day. Not losing them so much as sending them away, banishing them. They vanished by my own hand. And for that, I may never be able to forgive myself. But I had to choose my child. Again.

Yet in between all that, the breakups, the letdowns, the entire days I suspected I might have fallen over the cliff into complete mental illness, in between those moments and the deadlines, Nisa and I would travel, as we do to this day, to places far and wide, in New York City where we live, or else across the country where friends live. We marveled together at the differences each place offered: the deserts of Southern California, the mighty mountains in the Berkshires; the ready dance, blues, and hues of Chi-town; the swaying palms and rainbow fish of Sanibel Island; the alligators and swamplands of South Carolina; and the hot, wet, greener than green of Mississippi.

And all that color and life everywhere, including in the parks and gardens of urban landscapes like our own. We lose ourselves, Nisa and I do, in art galleries and museums, in Marsalis's jazz and fifties rhymes, in movies and on Broadway, at the ice-cream stand in summer and our sushi spot all year long. We make intricate plans for the trips we have not yet taken together to Paris, the Eastern Cape of South Africa, and Bora-Bora. She wants to climb the volcano I climbed in

Costa Rica three months before I became pregnant with her. I promise her we will do that trip, and also one to Baja some January during the migration of the gray whales.

We embrace it, this life, bathe ourselves in it, retain the memory in stories we whisper to each other when it's late and dark but we want, still, to hang on. That's how I do it, I tell my sister, or anyone else who asks.

3.
The Enemy Within Dan Savage

There was no guarantee that doing an open adoption would get us a baby any faster than doing a closed or foreign adoption. In fact, our agency warned us that, as a gay male couple, we might be in for a long wait. This point was driven home when both birth mothers who spoke at the two-day open-adoption seminar we were required to attend said that finding "good Christian homes" for their babies was their first concern.

But we decided to go ahead and try to do an open adoption anyway. If we became parents, we wanted our child's biological parents to be a part of his life.

As it turns out, we didn't have to wait long. A few weeks after our paperwork was done, we got a call from the agency. A nineteen-year-old homeless street kid—homeless by choice and seven months pregnant by accident—had selected us from the agency's pool of screened parent wannabes. The day we met her the agency suggested all three of us go out for lunch—well, four of us if you count Wish, her German shepherd, five if you count the baby she was carrying.

. . .

We were bursting with touchy-feely questions, but she was wary, only interested in the facts: she knew who the father was but not where he was, and she couldn't bring up her baby on the streets by herself. That left adoption. And she was willing to jump through the agency's hoops—which included weekly counseling sessions and a few meetings with us—because she wanted to do an open adoption too.

We were with her when DJ was born. And we were in her hospital room two days later when it was time for her to give him up. Before we could take DJ home we literally had to take him from his mother's arms as she sat sobbing in her bed.

I was thirty-three when we adopted DJ, and I thought I knew what a broken heart looked like, how it felt, but I didn't know anything. You know what a broken heart looks like? Like a sobbing teenager handing over a two-day-old infant she can't take care of to a couple she hopes can.

Ask a couple hoping to adopt what they want most in the world, and they'll tell you there's only one thing on earth they want: a healthy baby. But many couples want something more. They want their child's biological parents to disappear so there will never be any question about who their child's "real" parents are. The biological parents showing up on their doorstep, lawyers in tow, demanding their kid back is the nightmare of all adoptive parents, endlessly discussed in adoption chat rooms and during adoption seminars.

But it seemed to us that all adopted kids eventually want to know why they were adopted, and sooner or later they start asking questions. "Didn't they love me?" "Why did they throw me away?" In cases of closed adoptions there's not a lot the adoptive parents can say. Fact is, they don't know the answers. We did.

Like most homeless street kids, our son's mother works a national circuit. Portland or Seattle in the summer. Denver, Minneapolis, Chicago, and New York in the late summer and early fall. Phoenix, Las Vegas, or Los Angeles in the winter and spring. Then she hitchhikes or rides the rails back up to Portland, where she's from, and starts all over again.

For the first few years after we adopted DJ his mother made a point of coming up to Seattle during the summer so we could get together. When she wasn't in Seattle she kept in touch by phone. Her calls were usually short. She would ask how we were, we'd ask her the same, then we'd put DJ on the phone. She didn't gush. He didn't know what to say. But it was important to DJ that his mother called.

When DJ was three, his mother stopped calling regularly and visiting. When she did call, it was usually with disturbing news. One time her boyfriend died of alcohol poisoning. They were sleeping on a sidewalk in New Orleans, and when she woke up he was dead. Another time she called after her next boyfriend started using heroin again. Soon the calls stopped, and we began to worry about whether she was alive or dead. After six months with no contact I started calling hospitals. Then morgues.

When DJ's fourth birthday came and went without a call, I was convinced that something had happened to her on the road or in a train yard somewhere. She had to be dead.

I was tearing down the wallpaper in an extra bedroom one night shortly after DJ turned four. His best friend, a boy named Haven, had spent the night, and after Haven's mother picked him up, DJ dragged a chair into the room and watched as I pulled wallpaper down in strips.

"Haven has a mommy," he suddenly said, "and I have a mommy."

"That's right," I responded.

He went on: "I came out of my mommy's tummy. I play with my mommy in the park." Then he looked at me and asked, "When will I see my mommy again?"

"This summer," I said, hoping it wasn't a lie. It was April, and we hadn't heard from DJ's mother since September. "We'll see her in the park, just like last summer."

We didn't see her in the summer. Or in the fall or spring. I wasn't sure what to tell DJ. We knew that she hadn't thrown him away and that she loved him. We also knew that she wasn't calling and could be dead. I was convinced she was dead. But dead or alive, we weren't sure how to handle the issue with DJ. Which two-by-four to hit him with? That his mother was in all likelihood dead? Or that she was out there somewhere but didn't care enough to come by or call?

And soon he would be asking more complicated questions. What if he wanted to know why his mother didn't love him enough to take care of herself? So she could live long enough to be there for him? So she could tell him herself how much she loved him when he was old enough to remember her and to know what love means?

My partner and I discussed these issues late at night when DJ was in bed, thankful for each day that passed without having the issue of his missing mother come up. We knew we wouldn't be able to avoid or finesse it after another summer arrived in Seattle. As the weeks ticked away, we admitted that those closed adoptions we'd frowned upon were starting to look pretty good. Instead of being a mystery, his mother was a mass of distressing specifics. And instead of dealing with his birth parents' specifics at, say, eighteen or twenty-one, as many adopted children do, he would have to deal with them at four or five.

He was already beginning to deal with them. The last time she visited, when DJ was three, he wanted to know why his mother smelled so terrible. We were taken aback and answered without thinking it through. We explained that since she doesn't have a home she isn't able to bathe often or wash her clothes.

We realized we had screwed up even before DJ started to freak. What could be more terrifying to a child than the idea of not having a home? Telling him that his mother chose to live on the streets, that for her the streets were home, didn't cut it. For months DJ insisted that his mother was just going to have to come live with us. We had a bathroom, a washing machine. She could sleep in the guest bedroom. When Grandma came to visit, she could sleep in his bed and he would sleep on the floor.

We did hear from DJ's mother again, fourteen months after she disappeared, when she called from Portland. She wasn't dead. She'd lost track of time and didn't make it up to Seattle before it got too cold and wet. And whenever she thought about calling, it was too late or she was too drunk. When she told me she'd reached the point where she got sick when she didn't drink, I gently suggested that maybe it was time to get off the streets, stop drinking and using drugs, and think about her future. I could hear her rolling her eyes.

She'd chosen us over all the straight couples, she said, because we didn't look old enough to be her parents. She didn't want us to start acting like her parents now. She would get off the streets when she was ready. She wasn't angry and didn't raise her voice. She just wanted to make sure we understood each other.

DJ was happy to hear from his mother, and the fourteen months without a call or a visit were forgotten. We went down to Portland to see her, she apologized to DJ in person, we took some pictures, and she promised not to disappear again.

We didn't hear from her for another year. This time when she called she wasn't drunk. She was in prison, charged with assault. She'd been in prison before for short stretches, picked up on vagrancy and trespassing charges. But this time was different. She needed our help. Or her dog did.

Her boyfriends and traveling companions were always vanishing, but her dog, Wish, was the one constant presence in her life. Having a large dog complicates hitchhiking and hopping trains, but DJ's mother is a petite woman, and her dog offers her protection. And love.

Late one night in New Orleans, she told us from a noisy common room in the jail, she got into an argument with another homeless person. He lunged at her, and Wish bit him. She was calling, she said, because it didn't look as if she would get out of prison before the pound put Wish down. She was distraught. We had to help her save Wish, she begged. She was crying, the first time I'd heard her cry since that day in the hospital six years before.

Five weeks and $1,600 later, we had managed not only to save Wish but also to get DJ's mother out and the charges dropped. When we talked on the phone, I urged her to move on to someplace else. I found out three months later that she'd taken my advice. She was calling from a jail in Virginia, where she'd been arrested for trespassing at a train yard. She was calling to say hello to DJ.

I've heard people say that choosing to live on the streets is a kind of slow-motion suicide. Having known DJ's mother for seven years now, I'd say that's accurate. Everything she does seems to court danger. I've lost track of the number of her friends and boyfriends who have died of overdoses, alcohol poisoning, and hypothermia.

As DJ gets older, he is getting a more accurate picture of his mother, but so far it doesn't seem to be an issue for him. He loves her. A photo of a family reunion we attended isn't complete, he insisted, because his mother wasn't in it. He wants to see her "even if she smells," he said. We're looking forward to seeing her too. But I'm tired.

Now for the may-God-rip-off-my-fingers-before-I-type-this part of the essay: I'm starting to get anxious for this slo-mo suicide to end, whatever that end looks like. I'd prefer that it end with DJ's mother off the streets in an apartment somewhere, pulling her life together. But as she gets older that resolution is getting harder to picture.

A lot of people who self-destruct don't think twice about

destroying their children in the process. Maybe DJ's mother knew she was going to self-destruct and wanted to make sure her child wouldn't get hurt. She left him somewhere safe, with parents she chose for him, even though it broke her heart to give him away, because she knew that if he were close, she would hurt him too.

Sometimes I wonder if this answer will be good enough for DJ when he asks us why his mother couldn't hold it together just enough to stay in the world for him. I kind of doubt it.

4.
Foreign Relations Suzanne Kamata

When I am four months pregnant with twins, my husband, Yoshi, says, "Let's get a divorce." We have been arguing over the prospect of moving in with his mother. She has been a widow for going on three years now, and to hear my husband tell it, she is lonely and depressed. As the eldest child and only son, he feels a filial obligation to take care of her. In Japan, tradition dictates that the eldest son remain in the ancestral home to take care of his parents. He and his wife are also responsible for the family shrine, which is dedicated to the spirits of generations of forebears who have passed on.

When I first came to teach English in Shikoku on a year-long program sponsored by the Japanese government, I heard about the hardships of wives of eldest sons—they were bossed around by their mothers-in-law, loaded with household chores, and their children didn't really belong to them, but to their husband's families. When I fell in love with Yoshi, an eldest son, I had misgivings about spending the rest of my life in Japan. But when he asked me to marry him, he assured me that we wouldn't be expected to live with his parents. Besides, true love conquers all, right? I accepted his proposal.

But now, Yoshi has changed his tune. A month after we signed the deal for a house of our own, my father-in-law was diagnosed with lung cancer. Another month later, he was dead, leaving my mother-in-law alone in her large house. Yoshi's Confucian ethics kicked in. Since then, he's been lobbying for us to move in with her.

As an American woman in rural Japan, I believe that living with her would be a recipe for disaster. And besides, I know that since the death of her husband, my mother-in-law has led an active social life. She learned to drive, and she's been attending a variety of adult education classes.

I think of my grandmother, who blamed her divorce in part on her live-in German mother-in-law. I can't imagine sharing a kitchen, a life, with my conservative Japanese mother-in-law.

"We can make a new kind of family," Yoshi argues.

"What's so new about the eldest Japanese son living with his mother?" I ask.

He tries a different tack. "You obviously can't adjust to Japanese customs. If you don't want to live with my mother, then you should go back to America."

I'm getting tired of fighting over this. If I'm the one standing in the way of his and his mother's happiness, then I'll step aside. "Okay," I tell him. "I don't want to make your life miserable. If you want a divorce, I'll give it to you."

He disappears for a few days, returning home only to sleep on the sofa at night. Finally, he comes to me, ravaged and sleep-worn, and says, "I'm sorry. I don't want a divorce."

We stop talking about breaking up and consider the immediate future. I tell Yoshi that I want to stay home with our babies. In my younger days, I'd thought that there was nothing I wanted less than to be a housewife like my mother. How boring, I'd thought, listening to my mother talk about the bargains she'd found that day at the grocery store. How unambitious. But now that I'm about to become a mother myself, I desperately want to be there for my children's early years. I don't want to miss a second of their development. I want to be on hand for their first steps. I can't imagine surrendering their care to anyone else—especially not to someone of another culture.

"My mother had a job when I was a baby," Yoshi says.

I know, I know. She worked all through his childhood as a hospital dietitian. In the early years, almost all of her salary went to day care, but she stuck it out and kept her place in the system. At the time of her retirement, she was the boss.

If I stop working, I won't be putting my career at risk. In fact, I am sick of teaching English to Japanese elementary school students—sometimes as many as thirty-eight first-graders in one classroom. My job offers no chance of advancement. I am a foreigner employed on a one-year renewable contract, and I've recently been informed that if I want to continue working, I'll have to go back to the beginning of the pay scale. I want to quit.

Still, there is the money issue. My salary is over half of our income. If I give up my job, we'll have to cut back on our expenses, and there will be no extras—no more trips to Singapore, no more wine-of-the-month club, no more cashmere sweaters.

Yoshi makes some noises about taking paternity leave, since my salary is higher than his. He's a high school PE teacher and has been recently become the baseball coach of a brand-new high school—a dream come true. The problem is, his team consists of eleven sophomores who are always threatening to quit. Baseball is a glamorous sport in Japan, but this school is geared toward academics, not athletics, and the parents are always complaining that batting practice is cutting into homework time. Every game, Yoshi's team is badly defeated. The scores: 20-0, 21-0, 19-1. Yoshi says that he is not a good coach and he wants to quit.

I admire Yoshi's forward thinking, and I believe that, yes, he has the right to take care of our babies for a year. But I want this parenting gig too. Full-time. We still have a few months to think about it, however. I've been granted fourteen weeks of prenatal leave and another eight of postnatal leave. That means we have until November to work something out. Or so I believe.

I go into premature labor at twenty-four weeks and am admitted to the hospital. I'm hooked up to an IV and my movements are restricted. I brush my teeth while on my back and eat my meals at a forty-five-degree angle. For ten days, my feet do not touch the floor. Even so, my belly continues to tighten with contractions, and blood stains the white sheets.

My parents call each morning from South Carolina and my mother-in-law drops by with washed pajamas and cream puffs. My brother-in-law's aunt comes by. "You shouldn't read," she tells me. "It excites the mind and is bad for your baby." She says that I should lie quietly and talk to my babies. For three months.

My husband comes every day after teaching high school PE and coaching baseball. He brings my mail. One evening, he brings a letter saying that one of my short stories, published the previous fall in a small literary magazine in Illinois, has been chosen by a famous poet for a literary anthology. I can't wait to tell my parents.

I'm starting to relax. I'm even beginning to enjoy myself. The doctor announces that I can start using the toilet again. The catheter is removed and I begin testing my shaky legs, taking my first tentative steps toward wellness.

The next morning, I wake soaked in blood. My roommates slept through my frantic call to the nurse. Soon, I lie on an operating table awaiting an emergency C-section. I am surrounded by Japanese-speaking strangers wearing blue gauze masks and matching smocks. Yoshi, called away from a baseball game, sits outside in a waiting room with my wedding ring in his pocket (no jewelry allowed during surgery). The rest of my family is thousands of miles away. I have lived in Japan for ten years, but it has never felt as foreign as it does at this moment.

Someone tells me to curl up in a ball. I ease onto my side and curl. I feel the needle slide into my spine. My lower body becomes warm and then quickly goes numb.

The obstetrician starts swabbing my middle with antiseptic. Another man, identified as the neonatal specialist, enters the room. "Twenty-six-week baby very difficult," he tells me in heavily accented English. "I will do my best."

I look at the clock. It's eight-thirty in the morning. I don't want to think about what is going to happen in the hours, days, weeks to follow.

Minutes later, the obstetrician slices open my abdomen and pulls out my son. I can't see what's happening because a screen has been set up over my chest, but I can feel the liquid ooze over my belly and the fishlike squirm of my two-pound baby boy. "*Kawaii*," the nurse holding my hand says. "He's cute." I hear his cry—a tiny mewling—and then he is whisked away.

"Now we'll go in for the other one," Dr. Maeda says. He quickly delivers my one-and-a-half-pound daughter, the one who has lived beneath my heart for six and a half months. And then she's gone too.

I lie on the table, resigned and passive. This was supposed to be one of the most joyous moments of my life, but I feel like a failure. Although I tried to do the right thing throughout my pregnancy—abstaining from coffee and alcohol, avoiding travel and smoky rooms—there is a chance that my babies won't make it through the next few hours.

Meanwhile, Yoshi's baseball team wins a game.

.   .   .

By some miracle, our twins survive. The following evening, I am wheeled to the NICU and I see my children for the first time. Their bodies are scrawny and red, but they have all ten fingers and toes. I can't see their eyes because they're fused shut. They have dark hair on their heads and soft hairs on their shoulders and faces. They both have little beards.

The neonatal specialist tells me that although there are many hurdles ahead, the babies are doing incredibly well. "Don't worry," he says. "Trust me."

After I am sent home, my mother-in-law insists on driving me to the hospital every morning.

"But they won't let you see the babies," I protest. In truth, I'd rather take public transportation. At least then I could be alone with my thoughts. Or I could read.

"I'll wait in the car," she says.

By now, it's summer. The mercury hovers around 90 degrees, the humidity is high. My mother-in-law waits in the car while I visit my children. Sometimes she gets out and sits under a tree.

"Why don't you go inside? You can wait in the hospital, where it's cool." I tell her that there is a sofa and soft drinks and a color TV in the waiting room.

"*Hazukashii*," she says. "I'm ashamed."

Ashamed of what? Of having sickly grandchildren? Of being noticed? Of taking up space? I realize once again that I could live here forever and not understand this country's people.

My son, Jio, is finally released from the hospital in August. His sister, Lilia, comes home in September, four months after her birth. Before we leave, the doctor tells us that we should avoid bringing our daughter to crowded places until she is at least two years old. He warns us that because her lungs have not sufficiently developed, a common cold could quickly turn into bronchitis or pneumonia or worse. He mentions the possibility of heart failure.

Lilia has never been outside the NICU before. The world must seem strange and scary to her, I think. Instead of all those sweet-tongued nurses in pink smocks, there are hulking, honking metal monsters. She cries in the car on the way home. I sing to her until she falls asleep.

Yoshi buys a musical mobile and little chairs that squeak when tiny bottoms sit upon them. He buys a stereo system just for the nursery so that our children can grow brilliant from Bach and Mozart, so that they'll be able to do calculus in kindergarten. "Only classical music," he insists.

Secretly, I play other kinds of music for them—madrigals, folk, the didgeridoo. With the babies in my arms, I dance around the room and bask in their smiles. I have always been able to derive energy and solace from music, but my husband devoted his youth to baseball and claims he doesn't have a favorite band.

When we bring Lilia to the pediatrician for a checkup, Yoshi says, "I don't think she can hear."

"But she stopped crying when I put on a CD," I say.

"Why don't we test her?" The doctor sets up an appointment for an ABR (auditory brain stem response test).

A couple weeks later, she is sedated and electrodes are taped to her forehead. Earphones are fitted over her head. A machine produces bleeps of up to 100 decibels, but my daughter's brain waves exhibit no response.

When I get home from the hospital, I crank up the blues. The music is too loud for babies—for hearing babies, that is—but Lilia is oblivious. She stares at her hand, a starfish swimming in the light. She doesn't move when I call out her name.

I spend the afternoon sobbing.

I call my family in South Carolina. My mother cries. I tell my brother, father of a healthy toddler, that I am grieving. "We're grieving too," he says. "But blind would have been worse." I'm not sure that I can agree, but I understand that I have my family's love and support.

I'm most concerned about my mother-in-law's reaction. A foreign daughter-in-law was bad enough. What will she make of a disabled granddaughter? On the other hand, by this time she has been rocking and feeding and changing Lilia for months now. Surely they've formed some sort of bond.

"She can have an operation later," my mother-in-law says. I'm not sure what she is talking about, but at least she isn't turning away.

. . .

Yoshi buys a Japanese book about deafness and I start reading up as well, in English. I order a couple of videos and master the alphabet in American Sign Language. I start signing with both of our babies. I read up on cochlear implants. I've never heard of this new technology before, but the possibilities excite me at first. I tell Yoshi about what I've discovered. A flap of skin behind the ear is cut open, and electrodes are placed in the otherwise useless cochlea. A speech processor worn outside the body sends electronic impulses to the electrodes inside, which are then conveyed to the brain. This enables profoundly deaf individuals to hear a simulation of speech. Most deaf people can hear only a limited range of sounds, and a hearing aid can only amplify those sounds, but with a cochlear implant a deaf person can have access to a wide range of sounds, from the low frequency of a boom of thunder to the high frequency of whistling. At first, Yoshi is skeptical. This operation is not widely performed in Japan.

We are referred to the Tokushima School for the Deaf, which serves the entire prefecture. Lilia is fitted with a hearing aid and we schedule training sessions starting in the fall.

Kimiko Nagao, the head of the early intervention program at the deaf school, is a competent and committed teacher. She is registered as a simultaneous interpreter of Japanese Sign Language and has many disabled friends. She knows about laws concerning the deaf in Sweden, about the latest happenings at Gallaudet University, and she has seen the deaf percussionist Evelyn Glennie in concert. She also seems to be against cochlear implants and believes that Lilia can hear well enough with just a hearing aid.

At fourteen months, Jio is walking and then running. Lilia continues to drag herself across the floor with her arms. She gets around well enough in a walker, but she is clearly delayed.

On a visit to the hospital, I happen to meet up with the neonatologist. I ask him if there is something wrong with her legs.

"Don't worry. She will make progress slowly, slowly." Such is the way of micro-preemies, he seems to be saying. And I am reassured. For a bit. After all, I am still coming to terms with my daughter's deafness. "Multiply disabled" would take more getting used to.

Lilia has been getting physical therapy at the deaf school, but no one has offered any sort of diagnosis. Then one day the school receives a special visit from a hotshot therapist. He offers to take a look at Lilia.

"CP, right?" he says.

"What?"

"She has cerebral palsy?"

"No!" I am deeply offended. I don't even know exactly what cerebral palsy is, just that it sounds awful and debilitating. I have an image of a drooling, contorted child. Lilia is not like that. Sure, her head tends to flop to one side, but she's beautiful. "She was extremely premature," I explain to the specialist.

We continue the therapy sessions, once a week, and Lilia continues to drag herself, mostly with her right arm, around the floor.

On our first visit to South Carolina with the twins, my father says, "There's something wrong with her. You'd better get her checked out."

Yoshi buys a book, one with pictures of children with pointed toes and clawed hands. Once we're back in Japan, we take Lilia to Hinomine, a center for the education and care of physically disabled children. After an examination lasting only several minutes, the doctor scribbles "suspected cerebral palsy" and prescribes therapy twice a week.

My mother-in-law tries to teach Lilia to walk by holding her upright as her little feet jerk and jitter against the floor. Whenever I see my mother-in-law doing this, I become annoyed.

She is obviously in denial, I think. Lilia's problem is not in her legs but in her brain. Even her physical therapist has said that "walking" her in this way has little meaning. She needs to develop not only strength but control.

In my heart of hearts, I know that my mother-in-law cares about Lilia and that she is just trying to help. And while I see my mother-in-law's intervention as a rejection of

Lilia's disability, I have to admit that I want my daughter to walk.

The months go by. Yoshi's reading catches up with mine. By this time, I have begun to learn Japanese Sign Language. I now know that there are many deaf people who have no desire to speak or hear, who are perfectly eloquent in sign language and comfortable in a culture of their own. But Yoshi has decided that Lilia should have a cochlear implant.

"But Nagao-sensei says that she can hear at fifty decibels with a hearing aid," I say.

Yoshi snorts. "I don't think so." He yells at our daughter, sitting there in her high chair, to demonstrate. "Lilia!"

She doesn't look, doesn't even move her head.

"Nagao-sensei is just trying to make the parents feel better. She's telling you what you want to hear."

I roll my eyes. This is a man who believes the Oliver Stone version of JFK's assassination.

"Nagao-sensei wants to protect deaf culture."

I disagree, but the point is moot. Since entering the world, Lilia has been in and out of the hospital several times already for respiratory infections. One day, a tiny trickle of mucus would come from her nose; by the next she'd be intubated in the ICU, hooked up to a respirator. She isn't healthy enough to have a major operation.

Later, after a tonsillectomy, after her lungs have more fully developed and she starts gaining some weight, tests reveal that Lilia is indeed profoundly deaf. It is determined that the steroids prescribed to help her lungs during her hospital visits temporarily improved her hearing. When the effects wore off, her ability to hear declined. At her healthiest, even with hearing aids, she can hear almost nothing at all.

I finally concede that Lilia should have a cochlear implant.

A year after the operation, Yoshi's baseball team, the team he put together from scratch, makes it to the final game of the summer tournament. He is interviewed on the radio and in print. Suddenly, he's a local celebrity. Major league scouts call with an interest in the pitcher that he personally recruited. His team winds up losing in the tenth inning by one run, narrowly missing the opportunity to participate in the national baseball tournament—the ultimate dream of every Japanese high school baseball player and coach. Everyone tells him, "Maybe next year."

I'm proud of his success and happy for him—after all, after the birth of the twins I gave up teaching and am now following my own seemingly impossible dream of becoming a published novelist—but I'm finding it stressful to raise a disabled child in rural Japan. Yoshi works seven days a week, twelve hours a day. My kids need more of their father, yet if he decides to quit coaching in favor of a position that allows him to spend more time at home, it will have to be his decision. And it doesn't look as if things are leaning that way. Now that he loves his job, he is no longer interested in being a stay-at-home dad. In fact, he has reverted to traditional ideas about gender roles. Even though are struggling financially he seems to relish the power of being the sole breadwinner. When I suggest that I go back to work to bring in some money and to get a break from the intensity of mothering preemies, he insists that the children need me at home.

As a solution to our money problems, Yoshi proposes that we sell our house and renovate his mother's larger house, adding a small annex for her, where she will be assured a bit of privacy. Our new dwelling will be accessible and a haven for our disabled daughter. There will be a ramp for her wheelchair. The doors will slide easily open. The wallpaper will be resistant to bacteria and mold. The floors, where Lilia tends to crawl, will be heated in winter, and there'll be bars on the walls that she can grab when she tries to walk. After his mother dies, Yoshi says, Lilia can live in the annex, where there will be a small kitchen and a bath. As a bonus, I will have my dream kitchen and a room for writing.

After five years of spending almost every waking moment devoted to my children with no real end in sight, I'm ready for some respite. Maybe living with my mother-in-law won't be as difficult as I imagined after all.

My daughter still can't walk and, although she's had an operation for a cochlear implant, she can't talk. She will obviously need me for a long time. At least my mother-in-law would be able to look after the kids for a small part of the day, long enough for me to make a run to the grocery store. And she'd be able to help Jio and Lilia with Japanese homework and occasionally babysit when Yoshi and I can arrange an evening out. Also, and perhaps most important, with my husband gone all the time, there's no one around to model Japanese for Lilia. If we live with her grandmother, whom she adores, Lilia will have an incentive to learn the language. So, after ten years of no, when Yoshi asks again, I finally say yes to living with my mother-in-law.

Blueprints are drawn up, and I begin to prepare myself. My mother-in-law, however, confides that she feels she is being pressured by her son to agree to the move.

I'm starting to wonder if mother and son truly understand each other. I've heard Japanese people say that they communicate via *inshin denshin*, which could be translated as "mind reading." Some people believe that because Japan is supposedly a homogenous culture, everyone thinks the same way and there is no need for words. Could it be that Yoshi is simply operating on cultural assumptions? He has been raised to believe that it is his duty to care for his aging mother, and she is of a generation that rarely speaks frankly.

"If you don't want this to happen," I tell her, "you need to talk to Yoshi yourself."

She nods. "I will."

A week or so later, she drops by in the evening, when he is sure to be home. I leave them alone behind closed doors to talk. I try to eavesdrop, but all I can hear is patches of silence, where I envision my mother-in-law, head down, shoulders hunched, as she makes her case in barely audible tones, followed by my husband's booming—angry?—voice.

After she's gone, I ask, "What did she say?"

He shakes his head in disgust. "She says that she doesn't want us to move into her house because she's afraid the neighbors will talk about Lilia."

"What?"

What would they say? I wonder. That she can't walk? That she is deaf? That she can't talk? All of these things are true, so why bother hiding them? I've read that, according to traditional Japanese belief, a child's disability is due to the sins of the mother. Is it possible that my mother-in-law's neighbors would think that we are tainted somehow? Could they be that superstitious at the dawning of the twenty-first century? Does my mother-in-law think that? If so, I figure they are all due for some enlightenment.

Just when it appears that the deal is off, my mother-in-law decides that she wants us to move in after all and construction begins. In the spring, when the renovation is almost completed, she drops by and says, "Let's try to have fun living together."

I give her a tight smile. "I'll do my best."

"I won't be around much longer. . . . "

She is in her sixties, with no life-threatening diseases. Her father lived to be almost one hundred. "Oh, no," I say. "Please don't say such a thing."

"If I do anything that you don't like, please tell me," she says. "Let's be frank with each other."

"Okay," I reply. But I don't invite her to criticize me.

Nevertheless, I decide that I will be on my best behavior. I will not complain to Yoshi about his mother. He won't turn into one of those guys who stays late at the office to avoid the bickering of his wife and mother at home. If something comes up, I will deal with it myself. Besides, she's been living on her own for ten years. She will continue living her life, and I will live mine. We probably won't be seeing much of each other at all.

Wrong. The first day of our cohabitation, a Saturday, she pops in every half hour. She is concerned when she finds that I have not yet prepared lunch, though it is noon. Never mind that she saw us eating a late breakfast.

By this time, my mother-in-law has abandoned her flower arranging, her pool exercises, and the class where she made strawberries out of dough. It seems that all of her attention is now directed at us. She scolds me for storing my broom in the entryway—bad form—and tells me that she'd rather I didn't walk to the grocery store, which is five minutes away on foot; please ride a bike or go by car because, well, the neighbors have mentioned it. Apparently it is best if one is never noticed at all.

Meanwhile, I try to keep my mouth shut. I'd like to ask her not to bustle over with a tray of tea and rice crackers every time I have a guest—I can handle hospitality in my own quarters—but I know that she means well.

My mother-in-law, like most women in Japan, has been raised to be attentive to others and to ignore her own needs. I, on the other hand, come from a DIY culture that encourages independence and treasures privacy. We are, it seems, at cross-purposes.

One day, when Jio has a fever, I ask her to babysit him so that I can take Lilia to school. I return home to discover that she has taken him to the store to buy snacks.

"Did you go by car?" I ask, thinking they may have walked.

"No," my son says. "We went on Obaachan's scooter."

I am suddenly livid. He is only six years old, and he wasn't wearing a helmet. Not to mention his fever.

"Don't ever do that again!" I tell my mother-in-law. "It's dangerous!"

She doesn't seem to know what I am talking about at first. I can't tell if she simply doesn't understand my foreigner's Japanese, or if she can't comprehend why a ride on the scooter would make me so unhappy.

After all, she was doing me a favor by looking after Jio. And she'd only meant to make him happy, to dote on him as she was unable, as a working mother, to dote on her own son when he was little. This is the way of grandmothers everywhere, is it not?

Or maybe she is exerting great self-control while being disrespected by a younger foreigner, her son's wife, the woman who was meant to be a sort of apprentice. Perhaps she had expected to teach me about child care and cooking and tending the family shrine. Instead, she is face-to-face with this bossy blonde.

She offers a vague excuse—"Jio wanted to ride on the scooter"—and doesn't speak to me for the rest of the day.

Later, my husband tells me that my mother-in-law's invitation of criticism was only a formality.

Although my mother-in-law courts Jio with sweets and toys, my son, who has memories of being dumped at his grandmother's house during Lilia's long hospital stays, tends to keep to our part of the house. I wonder if he has overheard me talking to my expat friends about my frustrations as a daughter-in-law. He is very sensitive to my moods and tone, so maybe he is showing his allegiance to me. Lilia, on the other hand, who cannot hear me mutter under my breath, seeks out her grandmother several times a day. She slides open the doors that separate our quarters and crawls down the corridor. She enters without knocking and makes herself at home. When she finds her grandmother, she launches herself at her knees, giving my mother-in-law what might be the tightest hugs she's ever had in her life.

Sometimes I wonder why I can't be more accepting of my mother-in-law. Why am I always irritated with her? Why am I always angry? I've managed to forge a relationship with her son, a man whose upbringing was very different from my own, and I have learned to embrace a daughter who is unlike any daughter I ever imagined, and who does not speak my language or share my culture. Could it be that, deep inside, I am angry about my daughter's disabilities, this society's insistence that a father's work comes before his family, and my frustrations at putting my personal ambitions aside for this consuming thing called motherhood? Is it possible that I am projecting all of that subsumed anger onto my mother-in-law?

.   .   .

One afternoon, about a year after we've moved in, my son decides that he wants to take down the laundry. While he is unpinning the clothes, my mother-in-law, who has never in all this time taken down my laundry, is suddenly there helping him.

"He can do it himself," I say. I can't help but think that she is offended by the sight of a boy doing what she considers women's work. She has told me before that men are "special."

But my son, ever the peacemaker, says, "It's okay."

From that day on, my mother-in-law starts taking down my laundry every day.

"Thank you," I say in an exasperated tone, "but I can do it myself."

"But I have nothing to do," she says. "I have lots of free time and you are so busy."

It could be worse, I think. I remember how, a few months earlier, she took it upon herself to tidy up in my absence, throwing away my favorite jean jacket in the process. I decide to let it go. She takes down the laundry every day until one day, she doesn't.

On that day, she tells Yoshi that she doesn't want to live with us anymore. Although I am not in on the conversation, my husband tells me that I am not the cause of her discontent. Or not the only one, at least. It seems that she feels her son is not giving her enough respect. Also, she doesn't like the way we are raising Jio. She feels useless and unwanted. She is going to move out into an apartment of her own. She wants us to sell the newly renovated house and go back to our previous house, which we haven't yet managed to sell.

At first, I am relieved. Living together has turned out to be the disaster I predicted and it's not even my fault. Or at least not entirely. Maybe if I'd been friendlier, if I'd sipped tea with her once in a while or sat down to chat, she would have been happier. I know that she is lonely, but I have been the opposite of lonely—always craving time to myself. I've been desperate to protect my privacy and my sovereignty over my children, and afraid of having my identity washed away by Japanese expectations. I can't change my personality to fit my mother-in-law's needs.

Now that we know it doesn't work, we can split up and settle into our own lives. But later I think of how devastated Yoshi will be. He is only trying to do what's best for the rest of us. And I dread the thought of having to tell Lilia that her number one playmate will no longer be around. She will be heartbroken. And on second thought, the idea of my mother-in-law, estranged from her family, lonely and miserable in her little apartment, makes me sad too. On a more practical level, we probably won't be able to sell our house in the current real estate market.

Yoshi has a talk with his mother and convinces her to stay. We decide that we will have a "family night" once a week, when we will all have dinner together. My mother-in-law will be able to spend time with us without feeling that she is interrupting or intruding in our lives. She will cook every other week, which will give her a sense of purpose—and me a break. Yoshi will come home from work early. He'll be able to spend time with our kids.

While I suspect there will be more conflict to come, I am heartened to learn that my mother-in-law feels she has options; none of us are stuck here; if we stay, we are in this house together by choice. At the same time, I realize that whether we live together or apart, we will always be connected by blood and our mutual history.

The same goes for Lilia. While I expect we will be responsible for each other in one way or another for the rest of our lives, I imagine the choices that my daughter will make in the future. Perhaps one day she will have a family of her own—a husband and children, or a group of caring friends who live together. Maybe they will be Japanese, maybe many different nationalities. Maybe they will be disabled, maybe not. Maybe she will live in another country. Until then, our job is to help Lilia expand her options, to open the door to the world for her as wide as we can.

We often have different ideas about what would benefit Lilia the most, but I know at my core that all of us are fighting for what we think is best for her and that we have all been changed by having her in our lives. Among other things, Lilia has taught us never to take anything about the body for granted, including the ability to breathe; that there is always something to laugh about; that there are worse things than being noticed by the neighbors; and that you don't have to be able to walk in order to dance. Perhaps most important of all, Lilia has taught us to open our hearts. Not just to her, but to one another.

Several months later, I return from my new part-time job as a college instructor, tired and relieved to find my mother-in-law clattering around at the stove. Tonight it's her turn to cook. My husband cuts out of baseball practice early to come home and play catch with Jio. When the food is ready, my mother-in-law ferries trays of pork cutlets (Jio's favorite dish) and clam soup to our part of the house. We all sit down together to eat a sumptuous feast, my mother-in-law between her two grandchildren.

During the meal, Lilia fusses over her grandmother, making sure that her water glass is filled. My mother-in-law pretends to steal a morsel of food from her plate, and Lilia erupts in hilarity. Although Jio is quiet, he polishes off his cutlet, to his grandmother's delight.

After dinner, Yoshi sets up the Wii bowling game—a gift from his baseball team's parents. We all take turns knocking down virtual pins. Lilia, who can't yet roll a real bowling ball down a real bowling alley, and my mother-in-law both get strikes. We cheer for each other and laugh. Sometimes, our family is like this.

5.
Counting on Cousins **Amy Anderson**

I come from what most people around here consider a huge family. In total, the house I grew up in contained five girls, five boys, and an ever-changing multitude of cats, dogs, rabbits, and other assorted creatures. And no, we're not Mormon. Nor are we Catholic, the next question everyone asks after, "Wow! Ten kids! Are you Mormon or something?" The only people I've ever met who don't think my family is weirdly enormous are my students from large immigrant families. After years of being the only person I knew with so many siblings, I'm now surrounded by young adults who are the sixth of fourteen kids, or the oldest of nine.

Being part of a family that was considered a local curiosity had its downsides, of course. Going out to dinner was a rarity; a large party with two adults and ten kids (even though we weren't truly all kids at the same time) was always seen as an imposition, to put it nicely, by the waitstaff.

Fitting everyone in could sometimes be tricky too. Once, on a family trip to Disneyland, two of my brothers had to take the train from Sacramento to Los Angeles because the family van didn't have enough seats for all of us to make the drive together.

We frequently attracted odd looks, too, partly because there were so many of us and partly because with three white kids, three Korean kids, three Brazilian kids, and one Guatemalan sister, people spent a lot of time trying to puzzle us out. Were we a group home? A foster family? A school? These were the guesses we heard; I'm sure there were others. These days, everyone has a cousin or a friend who has adopted a baby girl from China, but twenty-three years ago, when my parents adopted their first Korean daughter, international adoption was relatively rare, and so strangers were perplexed by why children of every hue were calling our white parents "Mom" and "Dad."

As an introverted person living in a crowd, I thought moving out and living with just one person (my boyfriend at the time, Kelly) would be heaven. In reality, the quiet of our little house terrified me. I had no idea how to be alone. I'd turn the TV on for background noise or go to coffee shops to study, having found that all my complaining about how my parents' house was too noisy and distracting for me to be able to concentrate might have been unfair. I'd never lived in such a small household. For the first few months we lived together, Kelly would wonder why I'd cooked an entire jumbo pack of spaghetti and two huge jars of sauce for the two of us.

While I've gotten better at gauging how much pasta to cook, I'm still learning how my ideas about life and parenting were shaped by being part of such a big family. When my stepson, Vincent, started school, for example, and had to take a lunch each day, my husband, Chip, horrified me by asking him each night what kind of sandwich he wanted. Did he want mustard on it? Cheese? A pickle? What kind of juice box would he like? I'd listen, gritting my teeth, until finally I had to say it. "Don't give him all those choices! What are you, crazy? You want to be asking three kids for their special orders for the next ten years?"

Chip, the only child of his parents' marriage and the much younger brother of three doting sisters, was equally appalled. "What? I'm just asking him what kind of lunch he wants. What's the big deal?"

Huh.

What *was* the big deal? After all, if Chip wanted to make Vincent's lunch to order every day, that was his decision. Making lunches for all the kids, a rotating household chore when I was growing up, wasn't quite the arduous task when "the kids" consisted of one first-grader. (Once our other two children started school and the number of lunches to be made increased to three, we did institute the "You get what you get and you don't throw a fit" rule, a decision made in perfect parental harmony.)

When our kids squabble, Chip and I often have opposite reactions. Since he grew up as the only small child in the family, he's somewhat horrified by the constant vying for the favorite couch seat and the endless races to be the first one to open the door that I view as part and parcel of life in a family. He has a positive view of the possibilities of intervention; surely, if he just explains reasonably why their fights are silly, they'll stop.

My perspective is slightly more resigned; I'll break in to lower the volume of the arguing, and I don't tolerate hitting or bullying of younger siblings, but ultimately I'm not going to expend a ton of energy trying to keep my kids from fighting with each other. (I do spend a lot of time thinking longingly of the much bigger houses my parents raised us in. I suspect it's slightly easier to ignore sibling rivalry in a big old rambling two-story bungalow than it is in an 1,100-square-foot 1950s house.) Rules and routines like the ones my younger siblings hated—oldest child in the car rides shotgun, for instance—are the lifelines for parents of multiple children. Yelling "That's enough!" and threatening timeouts and/or the loss of certain privileges is also a strategy I'm willing to employ when necessary.

For better or worse, though, my kids aren't growing up in a family like the one I grew up in. I don't have it in me to parent ten kids—God knows my respect for my parents increases every day as I struggle to manage three. There is much to like about having a smaller family. For one, money and time are not quite as scarce. Financial stability, while unromantic, goes a long way toward decreasing stress on a marriage. Being able to spend one-on-one time with each kid and have a little left for myself is also a good thing; while my mom managed to make time for all of us, she did it by sacrificing her free time, as well as her sleep. I honestly believed, for years, that all parents slept about four hours a night, because that seemed to be the average amount of sleep my parents got when I was growing up.

But sometimes I look at my kids and wonder about what they're missing, and whether they're a little spoiled. They'd hasten to disagree, and compared to many of their peers' families we live a somewhat spartan life, but they've never shopped at the Canned Food Outlet, and they get new clothes from Old Navy and Target—sometimes clothes that aren't even on sale, for God's sake. They each have their own bedroom, something most of my siblings had to leave home to get, and we're hopeful, barring any catastrophes, that we'll be able to help them through college. And you can't begin to imagine what Christmas and birthdays look like around here, given that our kids are the only grand-children so far and have thirteen aunts and uncles, not to mention several great-aunts and great-uncles and three great-grandparents, all of whom like to shower gifts upon our household.

There's also the overwhelming whiteness of this little family of ours. I spent my first few years as a stepmother and mother secretly grateful that we looked just like many of the other families in the neighborhood. That odd mixture of shame and relief at not having to explain my family to curious bystanders was a new feeling for me. We live in California, and my kids go to public schools, so they're not going to live in ignorance of all other ethnicities and cultures, but they also won't be living with sisters and brothers whose first languages and skin color are a daily reminder that the world is much, much bigger than our little pseudo-suburban neighborhood.

Early on, adjusting to my role as the stepmother of then-toddler Vincent, whose schedule back then meant he spent every night and weekend with us, also left me shaken. I'd come into Vincent's and Chip's lives with the idea that blending families works the same whether we're in adoptive families or stepfamilies. I was not anything close to a cautious optimist; I thought I'd be the fairy godmother who came in and made this man and this little boy's life warm and fuzzy and full of homemade cookies and story times. I was a lot wrong and a little right.

While I dismissed those gloomy books about blended families with their warnings that "all blended families are born out of loss," just as I'd tried not to think too hard about the biological parents my adoptive siblings had lost, it turned out I couldn't ignore those losses, those ways that our little family was different from our neighbors', with two biological parents and two kids.

For instance, there was the issue of how I referred to Vincent. Would I tell a parent at the park who asked how old my son was, "He's two, and he's my stepson"? That seemed like overkill, but if I didn't clarify our relationship, I felt like I was trying to pass as his mother—an idea that made me very uncomfortable, given the very real presence of his mother in his life. Plus, Vincent calls me by my first name, and always has, so the minute he said my name, most people figured I was the nanny.

I found myself referring to him as "our two-year-old" when making small talk with the grocery-store clerk or a fellow parent at a park where I knew I wouldn't be spending much time. Eventually, I got comfortable with "stepmother" and "stepson." They're clunky words with some fairly awful connotations, but they're honest. I am his stepmother—not his "other mother" or his buddy or his nanny. I'm the woman who married his dad after his parents split up.

I'm also the woman who has cared for him for large chunks of time since he was a toddler. I'm the one who asked the pediatrician, at yet another visit to get some antibiotics for the ear infections, which seemed to be nonstop for a few years, about ear tubes. I'm the one who came home, told Chip what the doctor had said, and then stepped back. Stepparents can't sign medical forms or make major decisions like that; he and Vincent's mom needed to take over from there. I'm the one who did the research about the magnet school he ended up attending for several years, but when I went to enroll him, the school secretary told me I'd have to send in one of Vincent's parents; stepparents can't sign school-enrollment forms. So pretending that I'm a parent, with no "step" in front of it, is pretty impossible. After ten years in this role, I'm okay with that.

When Henry, my first baby and Vincent's first sibling, was born, I spent a few months having to rewrite my history. My thinking about adoption and about stepparenting changed as I birthed, nursed, and held this baby for hours (and hours and hours). Suddenly I felt ashamed of how much I'd presumed when I came into Vincent's life. Who was I to think he'd instantly love me the way he loved his parents? I'd missed so much of his life, and of Chip's evolution into fatherhood.

I also spent a few years being horribly judgmental. How could Vincent's mom have left? How could she stand being away from him at night? Henry couldn't seem to sleep without me nearby; what kind of mother leaves her baby and lets others take over? My adoptive siblings' stories seemed tragic in a way I hadn't seen before, especially as I immersed myself in attachment parenting. I started doubting my role in Vincent's life, and I felt enormous guilt about how uncomplicated and pure my love for Henry seemed compared to my love for Vincent.

Fortunately, I made my way out of what I came to call "the mommy cult," the school of thought that stresses the primary importance of a mother's total availability to children, when I was so sleep-deprived and martyred that no one, including myself, could stand me anymore.

Having my second baby helped too; suddenly, that "uncomplicated and pure" love I'd felt for Henry became more complex as I saw him next to this needy and tiny infant. What I'd thought was proof that I was a terrible stepmother turned out to be related to biology in a way I hadn't predicted: it seemed instinctual to care for the smallest, weakest member of the family first and let "the boys," as I found myself calling Vincent and Henry, become a little more independent.

And finally, focusing on the mother-child dyad instead of the whole family wasn't the way I grew up, and it wasn't how I wanted to raise my kids. Henry and Josie weren't being raised by just me; they were part of a family that included Chip and Vincent and, to a certain degree, Vincent's mom and partner and eventually their little girl.

I think now that I found comfort in the absolutist thinking of attachment parenting because I was so terrified of screwing up as a mother. Being a stepmother had already been harder than I thought it would be, and my own parents, who I'd thought would be the rocks (and free babysitters) I could count on, were going through a truly awful divorce, complete with restraining orders and siblings estranged from one or both parents. I needed to believe that if I followed one path, I'd be okay.

That's just not true, as all parents learn. But despite my missteps as a stepmother and the dissolution of the family I grew up in, I've come to value what I've learned from being part of both kinds of families.

From seeing my adopted siblings grow and thrive after less-than-ideal infancies and early childhoods, I've become a firm believer in the resilience of children, while at the same time adamant that those early losses matter and should be acknowledged. I've learned from Chip's stories of growing up with a stepfather and from what I know of his father and stepmother. I've grown from the painful restructuring of my relationship with my parents and siblings, as the dust has settled after the divorce. I've learned that blended families, like adoptive families, look different from the inside, even if not from the outside. Birthdays and holidays are painful. They just are. There is always someone missing. Sometimes it's because the adults involved can't be in the same room together. Sometimes it's because of geography. Why doesn't really matter. It hurts, and it sucks, and in many cases, that's going to be true forever.

Having been, briefly, a stepdaughter, during my mom's short marriage to her second husband, has made me more aware of the myriad ways Vincent feels torn between two families, no matter how hard we all try to get along. It strengthened my resolve to be kind, to be patient, not to push my own agenda without giving others a chance to catch up to changes. (It did not give me any magical gift of being able to actually *be* kind and patient at all times, but I'm trying, damn it.)

It turns out, too, that much of what I learned each time my parents added a child to our family applies to stepfamilies as well. When Meghan arrived here from Korea at age four, for instance, she spoke no English and we spoke no Korean. Singing children's songs together and laughing at cartoons were ways to communicate without language at first. I pretty much took that identical approach when I first met Vincent. Sure, we shared a common spoken language, but we weren't yet a family, just as Meghan (and Karin, Eric, Alex, William, Taina, and Catherine) and I weren't a family the second we met. Becoming family takes time. (We joke, though, that Karin became family driving home from the airport after we'd met her plane from Korea. We fed her McDonald's french fries, and she laughed and ate. It's possible that I remember this in a less realistic way than my mother might, but it seemed like Karin's transition took about two minutes.)

Practicing patience, acknowledging that adjustment takes time and will inevitably result in some difficult moments, and realizing that every small change has unpredictable ramifications for the whole family all help. This was true when I was growing up, and it's still true today.

My worries about my kids growing up in a smaller (and much whiter) family seem silly at times, since they are growing up with those sisters and brothers of mine as their aunts and uncles. Despite all my teenage complaints about having to babysit my younger siblings, I've been repaid beyond measure by those same siblings' willingness to care for my children. During Henry and Josie's baby and toddler years, my sisters Meghan and Karin were both college students. Despite having other jobs and busy class schedules, they were my kids' first regular babysitters during the afternoons when I was teaching. When my brother Matt was working on his master's degree, he put in hours as the most overqualified babysitter my kids have ever had.

Leaving my very young children with people who love them as much as I do was an enormous relief to this anxious mother; my kids cried when I came home from work, not when I left, because they knew that when I showed up, that meant the fun auntie or uncle they'd been playing with would probably go home. That feeling that family is a vast and loving resource is what I hope my children will have. Chances are they'll move away from this town all but a few of my family members still live in, and maybe Henry will babysit Vincent's young children someday in the future, but realistically, I know the chances are slim.

Despite Josie's pleas, I'm not willing to add a fourth child to our stretched-to-the-limits family. I'm banking on the promise of cousins, many, many cousins, in my kids' near future. (I'm also a little worried about Christmas—will we be renting an arena to fit everyone in? Seriously. These are issues big families who live in small California houses grapple with. I've heard of families who rotate which group gets to spend Christmas at Grandma's each year because they can't all fit at the same time.)

So I go along, trying to help Chip figure out how to raise more than one kid, and he helps me try to figure out how to live in a stepfamily. We'll celebrate ten years of marriage this summer by getting on a plane on our anniversary, all three kids in tow, to meet his dad and stepmother in Italy. There are, it turns out, all kinds of benefits that come with blended families.

6.
The Look ZZ Packer

I was prepared, but not as prepared as I should have been.

From the time my son was born until he was six months old, I got "the look," the look meaning, "Is that your child?" Sometimes people would ask me this outright: "He's not yours, is he?" When I answered yes (why else would he be tearing down my blouse and ogling my milk-enhanced cleavage?) they invariably made some sort of genetic calculation—this very dark African-American woman in front of them had somehow coupled with a Viking and produced this plump white child. *How odd!* Still, you could see, it didn't seem to quite make sense to them. Black women are supposed to have black babies. Or be paid to care for white ones. The idea of a black woman with a white-looking baby that was her own went against the laws of physics, genetics, social science—astronomy, it seemed. It forced imaginations back to the primal scene—"In order for her to have this baby she'd have to have had sex with a white . . ."

It was easier for them to simply assume that I was the nanny.

And my general appearance didn't dispel the notion. My

hair perpetually in a ponytail or braids, my face annoyingly, preternaturally youthful, so that people had always assumed I was eighteen when I was twenty-eight, and now that I was thirty-three with a child on my hip, I barely looked twenty-one. Perhaps that's why I was privy to a great deal more nanny-scolding than genetic confusion.

"His mother didn't give you a jacket for him?"

"I am his mother. And his jacket's right here." *His jacket's right here, bitch,* I wanted to say, abandoning my protofeminist hatred for that word in favor of simplistic maternal dominance. The screed would form in my head as the designated Produce Section Baby Adviser in front of me began plastering on her embarrassed smile—*You think he can't be mine? What's wrong with you! We're in fucking California where everybody fucks everybody else! At my pediatrician's office there are half-Eskimo, half-Ethiopian kids, so what's so odd about me being the mother of this screaming white-skinned, pink-cheeked baby!*

I'd heard of similar scenarios: the black woman nursing her very fair-skinned interracial child, only to be asked, by a white woman, "Do you get paid extra for that?" My neighbor and friend Nicole, herself interracial (though appearing more black than white), would go shopping with her blond-haired, gray-eyed boy, constantly pelted with looks that suggested she'd kidnapped the kid for her own nefarious purposes.

Another friend, Susanne, is Chinese-American and married to a Jewish man; their beautiful son, Kofi, looked markedly white for the first year of his life. Whenever Susanne walked Kofi through Central Park, she regularly got pleas from white women, desperate for a nanny who could teach their children Mandarin, or a nanny who would be a "strict disciplinarian." She was just thankful no one expressed an interest in a "nanny who'd be good in math." It simply didn't occur to any of these women that the white-looking child before them might be Susanne's own, or how offended they'd be if she walked up to them and foisted her number on them, bargaining interview times and pay scale before they got a word in edgewise. "If an alien were to walk through Central Park," the joke goes, "it would assume all babies started out white, then as they got older, became black or Chinese or Guatemalan."

The problem, as I see it, is that even on the relatively enlightened East and West Coasts, people still segregate their minds, even as their neighborhoods and social circles grow more integrated. Whereas I truthfully say that I don't think I experience overt racism when I go to get my daily nonfat latte here in the San Francisco Bay Area, I do experience another level of curiosity and wonderment when I do so with Donovan. Something elemental in people seems to assume that despite the baby's father being one race and the mother another, the baby will always come out looking like the parent standing right in front of them.

"Wow. He's so cute. He must look like his dad."

What to say to that?

A friend of mine, who is Korean-American and herself engaged to a half-Moroccan, half-Irish British national, said, "It's hard to believe he came out of you!" Not so hard to believe if you struggled to push all seven pounds, seven ounces out for hours nonstop, no epidural in sight, until he arrived a bloody mess, hoisted to your breast before you had time ask for more ice chips.

Perhaps most interesting is the reaction of black folks. A simple trip to the supermarket with my son Donovan in his Baby Björn became an invitation for black men to stare: *So, you gave up on the brothers, did you?* Or for black women to touch his straight hair and declare, "It's good hair now, but it'll nap up before you know it."

Sometimes I wonder if black people thought he was cute simply because he truly is a gorgeous baby, or because generations of conditioning have trained most blacks to believe that light skin and relatively unkinky hair are desirable. I always thought it strange how many old-line black folks in the South praised kids with light skin and straight hair as "beautiful," only as long as the kid was "black," meaning that neither parent was fully white. No one wants to think about a white parent being in the mix.

When Donovan turned six months old, he was diagnosed with ptosis, an eyelid disorder that usually results in one eyelid having no folds whatsoever. With most cases of single-eye ptosis, the kid looks as though he's been punched in the face, one eye swollen shut, or, in milder cases, ptosis can give the effect of the child perpetually squinting to see something in the corner of his vision. In Donovan's case, both eyes were ptotic, which meant that he simply looked as though both eyes were closing, as if he was always on the verge of sleep. Some people, though, thought he was Asian, or Filipino, and the questioning looks morphed from the previous "Are you the nanny" sort to "Who's *this* kid's daddy?"

At around ten months, more and more people began to wonder if Donovan's father was Asian, Filipino, or Hispanic. And then, around eleven months, something happened. Donovan started walking early—very early—and was booted out of the infant section in his day care and promoted to the toddler section. Instead of going three days a week, he now went four or five days a week, but the big difference with the toddler section was that they played outside, three or four hours a day.

Donovan would have most likely turned brown anyway—even before he began walking, his skin morphed from his dad's pale Irish-Hungarian tone into a more dusky gold. But the first week was dramatic. It all came together: the hair—a crop of beautiful curls—the nose—a little flat button, and those lips, lips Angelina Jolie would kill for—were all now offset by an incredibly round and decidedly bronze little face. Donovan's "negrescence" was now complete.

"He used to look like Mike," my friend said. "Now he looks like you."

I began to wonder if this was true. As far as I could tell, he looked the same as he did when he was six months—only older, darker, and with curlier hair. The features were the same. The coloring and hair tipped him over the edge.

"Oh, he's a brother, now," my friend said. "A little mixed brother, but a brother nonetheless."

I felt, I think, relief.

But it bothered me to feel that way. Why had these seemingly well-meaning people made me feel as though something was wrong with having this beautiful kid, with having a husband who wasn't my race? Why had my *not caring*

become a crime, and when I had a kid who visibly represented how I felt about interracial relationships—my decision to marry a white guy, his decision to marry me—so
many people who previously wouldn't have dared comment
found it their right to?

My refrigerator is my testament to just how mixed up it is
out here in San Francisco-land. I've collected pictures from
all my friends, all of whom seem to be popping out babies
like it's the end of the world. There's my son, with a black
mother and an Irish-Hungarian Cajun father. There's the
baby whose dad is black and whose mom is Vietnamese, the
baby with the Chinese-Welsh mother and the black dad,
the baby with the Jewish-black mom and the white dad, the
two girls with the Chinese-Hawaiian dad and the English-
German mom. There's the half-Persian Iranian, half-Scotch
girl and the half-Lebanese, half-Finnish boy with an Italian
last name. Then there are two "all white" kids and two "all
black" kids.

They are all American. All except one. One of the "white"
kids was just adopted from Russia, and my (white) friend
had sent me a picture of herself, holding her new son at last.
Another friend came over to my house, looked on the refrigerator, spotted the picture, and said, "Cute kid. Looks just
like his mom."

7.
Like Family Min Jin Lee

A little over a month ago, my nine-year-old son, Sam, and I moved to Japan. His father, Christopher, had already pitched camp in Tokyo in a corporate rental ten months prior to our landing. I have to tell you that I did not want to come here, though it made sense for Christopher's job and for my job, since my next book is set in Tokyo, and Sam yearned to live in the provenance of Transformers, Pokémon, and Yu-Gi-Oh! I was anxious about many things: not speaking the language, the history of discriminatory practices toward ethnic Koreans in Japan, and losing my beloved life in New York. Our sunny friends tried to show me the bright side. The harder they tried, however, the more I refused to listen. I would all but jut out my lower lip, wanting to say, *You don't understand.*

As if to prove my absurd New Yorkness, I went to see my therapist about this right before I left. I have been in therapy for about three years, and my shrink has helped me through scrapes and some near scrapes. He asked me what I would miss the most about New York.

I sat up straight on his lumpy brown sofa and gave him my three-part answer.

"You, my church, and Rosey."

My shrink appeared puzzled, and he assured me that he was only a phone call away, and there were churches in Tokyo. I knew that. But he hadn't said anything about Rosey. By this time, I had known about the decision to go to Japan for many months. In this period, I had been slowly letting go of people and places in my mind. I had been able to do this, because I knew I would return soon enough. Christopher promised that it wouldn't be permanent. The gift of being almost forty years old and having raised a child who will be ten presently is that I have learned that the quick passage of time is a guarantee.

In my therapist's office, I had not mentioned a fear of losing my mother, father, two sisters, brothers-in-law, or nieces and nephew, because I didn't have one. I belong to one of those families that does not speak to or see its members as often as we should, but if someone needed anyone to fall on a sword for her, there would be a queue waiting to commit the deed. As ever, I would be there for them, and they would be there for me. I would visit; they would visit. My friends would be constant too. When you are a New Yorker, you get used to finding new people and people going away. You realize that you will see nearly everyone eventually.

My shrink was right: I would be able to see him whenever I was in New York, and contact him via e-mail or phone. And God. Well, I was least troubled about Him, because I continue to believe what I learned in my confirmation class from Mrs. Novak when I was thirteen: God is defined by the three Os—omniscience, omnipresence, and omnipotence.

God would find me, and I would find a church in Tokyo too. But Rosey. I did not know what would happen, because she was someone who worked for me.

Christopher and I had our son at the end of January 1998. He was working as a junior salesman at a bank, and I was a former lawyer who had been trying to write fiction for three years. In connection with my difficult pregnancy and a long-standing liver illness, I developed a few ailments: a bruised tailbone, chronic bilateral tendinitis, and, more serious, liver cirrhosis. By May 1998, Sam was almost five months, and physically, I was not a well mother. My husband thought we should get some help. I mention that it was his idea because I did not think I needed any help. We didn't have much money or space, and I thought I could manage. Once Sam was sleeping, I had reasoned before he was born, I'd be able to cook, clean, mother, and jot a bit of a novel here and there. Sam came, but I also got sick. Motherhood isn't supposed to be easy, I thought, and when it wasn't, I figured it would gradually get better. Then Christopher said one day, "You're always angry." That was not pleasant to hear.

The next day, I went to the bookstore. When I have a problem, I reach for a book. At the Lenox Hill Bookstore, I bought a copy of *City Baby*—a reference guide for New York parents. I phoned an agency listed in its pages, and the next day, Rosey came by.

When Margaret Rosita Grandison arrived at our tidy two-bedroom apartment on Seventy-second Street, she was forty-seven years old and I was twenty-nine. It was the middle of

May. She wore a short-sleeved print blouse and a black skirt. Rosey's unlined complexion was medium brown, her dark hair straightened with a perm and styled modestly, and on one of her front teeth there was a decorative gold cap that she later had removed. She was from Bridgetown, the capital city of the island of Barbados. Her manner was guarded but warm, and her speech was polished. She did not talk too little or too much. When she smiled, her face expressed a girlish prettiness.

Like me, Rosey was a naturalized citizen. She was married to a welder; they had a married accountant daughter and a grandson. Rosey and her husband owned a single-family house in Brooklyn. Right away, she said she was only considering part-time positions because she was in line for a union job at a downtown hospital. She intended to have two jobs: one as a part-time babysitter and another as a hospital office cleaner—the latter giving her the kind of employee benefits that few household positions could offer. Rosey's competence and good judgment were evident. I wanted her approval.

She handed me a letter of reference from her most recent employers, who'd moved to London. I asked her questions cribbed from *City Baby*. We played this game: two immigrant women in a room—prospective employee, prospective boss—measuring each other. Could we live together? I didn't know it then, but certainly, that's what it would amount to for sixteen hours a week: Sam, Rosey, and me, and 968 square feet of New York real estate.

There was the issue of my lack of experience. I was a new mother and a new employer. In contrast, Rosey was a veteran babysitter. In my two brief years as a corporate lawyer, I could hardly ever get secretaries to do what I asked.

I hazard guesses as to why I was such a lousy person to work for: I was an immigrant with a foreign name that tripped people up, also over two decades younger and more educated than the middle-aged white women from the outer boroughs. Telling these women what to do was like ordering around my close friends' mothers from my old neighborhood, and frankly, I was terrible at it. I never felt like anyone's boss. Then again, would a young, Korean-American female secretary listen to me? Probably not.

So, I had not been graced with natural leadership skills; nevertheless, race, immigration, class, and religion invariably informed my work and life.

My deeply Christian parents taught my sisters and me to be good servants—to never be ashamed of honest work, because life could always change your station with a war, job loss, illness, or bad weather. In my youth, I had sold books, shoes, clothes, and costume jewelry, and I had taught unruly kids how to take the SATs. I have worked unreasonable hours as a junior lawyer while performing nonbillable tasks like ordering coffee and lunches, photocopying, keyboarding, filing, mailing, and pasting address labels when secretaries and paralegals couldn't or wouldn't help me, because I figured that was just how it was for people like me. I was new to this white-collar work—in more ways than one—and I decided to put my ego aside. It is worth remarking that I often defer, not always because I am so humble or humbled, but because sometimes, just doing that which needs doing is the easier thing. A pleaser is by nature a conflict-dodger.

If anyone would actually work for me, among other things, she would have to be self-motivated and principled. It would be preferable, too, if she could read my mind.

Rosey and I spoke for less than an hour and when she left, I phoned her reference in England. The reference said they were very sad that she wouldn't leave New York and work for them in England: "If Rosey will work for you, you'll have won the lottery." That day, I offered her the job: four hours a day, four days a week—sixteen hours total. Ten dollars an hour. She started immediately, and as of last month, Rosey has worked with us for nine years and three months.

My parents, two sisters, and I immigrated to America in 1976. In Seoul, my North Korean father had worked as a marketing executive for a cosmetics company, and my South Korean mother taught piano to neighborhood children in our home. A war refugee, my father was fearful of South Korea's political instability. Our immigration was sponsored by my mother's older brother, Uncle John, and when my father was forty-two and my mother was thirty-five, they arrived at Kennedy Airport with us three girls, ages ten, seven, and five. We moved to Elmhurst, Queens, and lived there for almost ten years before my parents crossed the George Washington Bridge to their American dream house in New Jersey.

In the States, my sisters and I did not grow up with babysitters or housecleaners. Six days a week, my parents worked together in a grimy wholesale jewelry store in Manhattan. My sisters and I went to the local public schools, and when we were younger, our mother left the store early, took the subway, and met us at home. In the evenings, our parents never left us with anyone else. In the mornings, they left before seven o'clock, and my sisters and I walked to school together. Date night—the occasional evening when married people romance one another—did not exist for my mother and father. Never once in my childhood did I see my parents dress up for a dinner out, attend a cocktail party, or pack suitcases for a weekend getaway—the entitlements of middle-class American married life. It did not seem strange to me then, because I had no contrary models except for books and television, but those stories were not about people I knew. As a child, I did not know if Korean parents did things for fun or personal fulfillment. My sisters and I saw our parents every night, and they saw us. If they might have preferred to be elsewhere, we did not know about it.

But back in Korea, things must have been different. I remember country girls who lived in our home. They were very young women who worked as maids and babysitters. There were two employed at all times, though with some predictable turnover—marriages or dismissals for negligence or stealing. I had to confirm their history with my family, because what I recall of them personally is at best shadowy. When Christopher suggested that we hire a part-time sitter, I had been resentful and anxious because I didn't want to leave Sam with someone who only thought of him as a job. I wanted someone who would love our child too. And could a person love a child only for money? Could anyone love for ten dollars an hour?

. . .

Rosey's life resembled my mother's more than my own. My mother, like Rosey, had to earn money. My mother was the second daughter of a prominent minister, educated at a first-rate university in Seoul, and she had studied music—a discipline that is still viewed by many in Korea as a luxury. My father was not a suitable groom according to my grandfather, who was proved right when, as a newly married man, my father turned out to be a temperamental employee and sporadic wage earner. As a result, my mother was forced to work as a piano teacher to generate a steady income for the family. But in order to have the time to work, my mother, like all working mothers who don't have a family member to watch their kids, had to hire others to take care of her children. There was also an unforeseeable benefit of her work: it freed me, when I became a mother, from any guilt of having another woman help take care of my child—my mother's labor and salary had supported our family, and so it became my experience of what women could choose to do.

In Korea, though, my mother was lucky: she loved teaching, and had found a way to be compensated for her passion. But eleven years into their marriage, my father asked my mother to go to America. As a boy, he had been a war refugee from the North, and in his early forties, he remained uncertain about the changing governments and the scarce educational opportunities, and he had his own dreams of the kind of mythical prosperity offered only in America. She did not want to go. They went anyway. For two decades, my mother and father owned a tiny shop in Manhattan where they sold gold-filled chains and brass earrings to small retailers from places like Caracas, Ibadan, and the Bronx. Unlike the store's two employees, who earned a modest wage, my mother, as co-owner, never drew a salary, her work contributing to the overall earnings of the store. There was very little to enjoy about her life at the shop. Sunny Variety Corp. was a corridor-shaped space of about 250 square feet; in the winters, it was intolerably cold, and my father used to wear two cardigans over his shirt and necktie and well-worn gray flannel trousers. My mother, who dealt with the customers, stood near the door with an electric space heater to keep her ankles warm. For breakfast, they ate bagels from coffee carts and split sandwiches for their lunch. They were held up at gunpoint twice, burglarized and mugged. My sisters and I cooked and cleaned the house, and took turns helping out at the store when school was out. In those years, we all did our best to manage.

Rosey and her husband, Ronald, had their only child in 1968. Their daughter, Yvonne, and I are only a few months apart in age. When Yvonne was nine years old, Rosey left her with a sister in Barbados to come to New York for work as a nanny. Rosey sent money for Yvonne's care and visited her regularly. Yvonne attended magnet schools in Barbados, and when she was sixteen, she joined her parents in New York, where she attended college.

That's how we began. This new person entered our home, and each weekday thereafter, Rosey and I worked beside each other. We were both immigrants, but somehow, I had ended up as her boss. I was intimidated because she could identify both croup and the Coxsackie virus, and Rosey didn't hesitate to tell me what Sam needed: friends, fresh air, and Vicks VapoRub. I did what she said, and I wrote her checks. It wasn't fair, but here it was: she was overqualified and underpaid relative to her skills, and I stood to gain from this inequity because there were enough immigrant women who needed jobs as babysitters in Manhattan. I paid her the going rate, and I tried to make sure that she was happy. This was my calculation: if Rosey is happy, then Sam will be happy, and if Sam is happy, then I am happy. We were a circle.

I don't know what she was like with the kids in her previous jobs, but I watched her with Sam every day. When I yelled at him for not having his sneakers on, anxious that he would be late for school, she called him darlin' and warned him with a look to get it together before the mother loses it again. When Sam refused to eat vegetables, she prepared chicken soup with butternut squash and green beans, straining it twice so he wouldn't see any trace of orange or green specks coloring the broth. If there were no frozen waffle sticks with dipping packets at the local Food Emporium, she bought them in Brooklyn on Sunday night and brought them for him on Monday morning. Sam asked Rosey to never leave us. That's the trap for babysitters—when you've fallen love with the child you're taking care of, you're never working just for the money. The more you become attached to the kid, the harder it becomes to treat the job objectively.

As Sam grew older and the demands of my illness increased, the nature of Rosey's job changed. In the beginning, it was Rosey who took Sam to the park, arranged play-dates, and kept him occupied for the sixteen hours when she was with him. When he started preschool, we both took him on his first day, and we both cried. He was fine, and we had to scoot away. On his fourth birthday, Rosey baked him a Thomas the Tank Engine birthday cake; she baked a Lego soccer field cake for his fifth.

Even though we had moved to a larger apartment below Canal Street when Sam was one, in a bizarre defiance of geography, we decided to send our son to kindergarten uptown. It took Sam forty minutes on the 1 or 9 train to get to school. Rosey would arrive at 7:15 a.m. to take him there. When she got to our apartment, Sam was supposed to have eaten breakfast, washed up, and be ready to go. Most days, I was up to the task. But when I wasn't, and Sam was not ready, Rosey took over. On such mornings, I felt grateful and humiliated. This was the unintended consequence of having Rosey in my life—she had come to know me too.

Sam's babysitter knew a great deal more about me than anyone else. She saw everything, because I worked at home. Rosey knew how long it took for me to shower, how long I talked long-distance to my friend Dionne when I was supposed to be writing or taking care of papers and bills, and how many cups of milky coffee I drank before I ate my large bowl of oatmeal at eleven o'clock. I didn't tell her any of these things—I didn't have to. When Sam was four, and when he began attending preschool from nine to three, and because of my liver illness, Rosey went from working sixteen hours a week to twenty-five hours a week, taking on the task of housework. She ended up spending a little less than an hour each morning taking Sam to school, another hour on the train including a quick stop at the market to pick up milk and juice, then did about three hours of housework. All told, she spent five hours a week with Sam and fifteen hours a week with me, his mother. Sam's sitter had become the sitter of both of us. When I began my six-month course of interferon B treatments for my liver, I knew for certain that I could not do without her. There was no one else who could take her place. When it came to Sam's happiness and welfare, I relied on her more than anyone else—she was constant relief.

Each morning, Rosey let herself into the apartment with her set of keys while I groused about in the kitchen fixing one of Sam's usual breakfasts—rice, toasted seaweed, and chicken, with a glass of orange juice. She would say good morning with her West Indian accent, and somehow, I would try to behave a little better, because it was like the good aunt had come to visit. Rosey made me want to be a better mother to Sam, because she was such a good mother to Sam. I never thought it was possible to compete with her, because she would have won surely, but I wanted her respect. If you asked Sam who his favorite people were, Rosey was always in his top three. Unlike me, she didn't shout or lose her cool. Rosey kept her word and never let Sam down. In a world where grown-ups fell short, Rosey raised our curve. Sam, a boy full of mirth and intelligence, maybe just came that way, but I believe that he learned to trust the world and to feel stronger about himself in part because of Rosey's guidance. She loved him and made him a better kid.

Rosey improved me too. When I first had Sam, for all the obvious reasons, I started to wear more wash-and-wear and jogging pants with elastic waistbands. Because we had so little extra money when I quit being a lawyer to write, I bought what I needed on sale. When Rosey started to do the housework, I noticed that my dirty clothes were returned to my closet laundered and ironed. I was surprised by this, because my clothes were inexpensive cotton things—things you wouldn't dry-clean or bother ironing.

Curious, I asked Rosey why she had ironed my clothes.

"Because," she said gently, "I want you to look nice—to look pretty when you go out."

My mouth made an O. Then it came to me: "Thank you," I said.

No one had ever taken the time to iron my clothes before.

When we first came to the States, my sisters and I wore hand-me-downs from our cousins. Then later, my younger sister and I wore clothes worn by our older sister when the sizes and seasons worked out. Before school started, our mother bought us new jeans and sneakers. We always had warm coats, mittens, and proper footwear—it's hardly a sad story. But, as a clergyman's daughter, my mother disapproved of vanity. My sisters and I were not encouraged to dress up, or to care much about our looks. As a child I had been the sort who sketched drawings of princesses in long, diaphanous gowns with trains. I was never happy wearing sensible turtlenecks and brown corduroys, but I sensed that it would have been wrong to ask for something beautiful and costly from parents who were just getting by themselves. And after I had Sam, something harsh and pragmatic within me had kicked in again, as if spending money on myself was a needless extravagance when I had a son, and I found myself choosing clothing with utility and modesty in mind. And when Rosey said she wanted me to look pretty when I went out, it was a surprise to hear such words. But I remembered my old self—the one who had dreamed of gowns and frippery. When she said this thing, I felt it was okay to want to look attractive again.

In the past ten years, I have heard sad and bad nanny stories, and I never know what to say, because the way I felt about Rosey seemed idealized. And yet, whenever anyone said, "Oh, our babysitter is like family," I would also feel uncomfortable, because that didn't sound wholly true. Would she come to work if you didn't pay her? Would you expect her to? I found that I couldn't talk to anyone about Rosey, because I didn't think anyone would understand.

Then my husband asked me to go to Japan and I knew we had to move.

When I told Rosey this, she was silent for a bit, but said it was the best thing for Christopher's job. I wanted to talk about it some more with Rosey, but I found that I couldn't.

"You will find someone else to help you," she said, smiling.

"No. No one like you." I shook my head in denial, because after having a child, Rosey was the best person I had come to know. She loved Sam, and in a way, it felt like she was loving me, because when my child was with her, I felt good, that it was possible for me to focus on something else, for me to do my other work, for me to be me again. It was a consolation—a gift.

Rosey looked away, and so did I, because we couldn't say much anymore.

Christopher had gone to Tokyo ten months ahead of us. He visited us regularly, but even so, it was a difficult time for our family. We have been married for fourteen years now, and in the year we lived apart, there were too many moments when I thought, This—this being married—is tough. He was my husband and the father of our son, but I felt that because we were a family, we were being taken for granted. Somehow, we had to accept these intervening moments of hardship and separation, because there was this longer commitment, these bonds we had forged with promises and history. Because we were a family, we were going to move to Japan. On our over-seas phone calls, I would get upset at Christopher, because so much of what was happening was too hard. He would say always, "We will all be together again."

After Christopher left, it was Sam and me, but it was really Sam, Rosey, and me, because she was, next to Sam, the person I saw more than anyone else. But I still couldn't talk to her about leaving. Every time it came up, I would be struck dumb, because I thought if I tried, I would start to cry and not stop. There were moments when I couldn't look at her, because it made me so sad to leave her. When my friends and family had this emotional response to me leaving New York, I would feel exasperated, because I knew I would see them again. Nothing would change except for the fre-quency of our meetings. And then I began to understand. I did not know what my relationship was with this woman I loved and needed who was, at the heart of it, also my employee. I have always wanted to be good at saying what needed saying; in my intimate relationships, I have sought clarity, but Rosey and I didn't have the words. I was afraid. I think I was afraid that she did not love me back.

About two months before we left, Rosey told me that she was taking some time off from her job at the hospital in November because she was going to come to Tokyo and help me unpack. All of our possessions had been shipped in a cargo container and would arrive then. It didn't matter that Christopher's company's agents would be responsible for unpacking everything; she wanted to be there. We both knew this.

"Min, I have to help you settle in," Rosey said.

"Are you sure?" I asked. "You don't have much vacation time."

She was certain that she needed to come. Of course, I wanted her to, but I had not asked. It would not have occurred to me to ask her to fly thirteen hours each way, endure jet lag, and spend her hard-won, union-determined vacation days. Also, I didn't know where I stood with her. Would she want to spend time with us when she did not have to? When I hadn't formally engaged her? Would she be like any other houseguest, or would she feel compelled to do all that she usually did for us when she worked for us? Would I pay for her time? Should I? Then I stopped myself with the questions, because it would make us so happy if she came. We would be happy to send her a ticket. Give her whatever we could. We would make it a holiday for her. Rosey had never traveled with us before. Maybe we could take a short trip while she was with us. Sam would be thrilled.

"I can come in November. I took the time off. For you and Sam." She was adamant.

I nodded, because then I understood how things were between us. She was trying to tell me that we wouldn't end just because we were moving. She wouldn't let that happen. It was her decision, and she wanted to see us again. The terms would change, but our relationship would continue. Growing up, I had wanted a mother and a father who said things like "I love you"—a phrase I heard television parents utter easily and every day. I never told anybody about this, and certainly not my own mother and father, who did little else except for provide for me. I know they would think that this wish to hear such words was foolish. Through their lives, I had come to learn that time and work were the costly goods, and words were, well, they were easy to give away. As an adult, at the cusp of another stage of life, I had met another person who loved without language. Rosey was coming to see us in Tokyo. She loved us back.

The day we had to get on the plane for Tokyo, Rosey was supposed to meet us for breakfast at a restaurant near our apartment. The night before, we had to sleep at a hotel because all of our things were packed up. That morning, I was feeling nervous about seeing Rosey for breakfast—this beautiful woman I had known for almost ten years. Someone I had seen almost five days a week for nearly a decade, some-one I had raised a child with.

At the restaurant, we ordered our meals, then I showed Rosey my calendar for the winter ahead, and asked her if she could make these dates and flights. I wanted to show her that she was in my life in the future. How could we start another life without her? We didn't need her help to settle in, but she and I needed an excuse, some sort of story to make sense of our relationship. If unpacking was our cover, well, that would do for now. Things would be different, because we would be different, and it would be okay if we fumbled, because we would be approaching each other.

It has only been five weeks, but each morning as Sam gets ready for school, I long for a key to turn and for Rosey to walk through the front door. When you miss a person, I think what you are saying is that someone else completes you. Our days are less without her, and we feel her lack. But she will be here soon. We will wait for her to come. We will all be together again.

8.
Daddy Donoring **Antonio Caya**

I met Sarah in 2001 on a photo shoot. She was nominally gay and I was straight and single, but after-work socializing (and drinking) led to dating. We liked each other, but it became clear pretty quickly that we weren't compatible. I drank a lot and was not a great communicator; she drank very little and liked to talk, a lot.

I wasn't looking for a relationship, and while she was still a little ambivalent about dating men at all, she leaned toward something secure, or at least well defined. We stopped dating after a few weeks but stayed on friendly terms, working together sometimes on shoots.

During those days, the idea of having kids together never came up. I had never wanted children, but always thought that would change. So I put all of my consideration of the matter on hold, in reserve, for the right person, for the right stage in life, for some sort of chemical reaction that takes place at a certain point in your thirties. I thought that I would evolve, that it would be organic and instinctual, that I would come around and it would all make perfect sense.

. . .

Two years after meeting Sarah, we had become good friends, and she asked me about being a donor in the course of a conversation. She was thirty-seven, the desire to have a kid was starting to consume her, and I suspect it took quite a degree of effort for her to make the pitch sound at all casual. She was back to dating women but struggling to make anything work, and during a phone conversation I joked with her about trying so hard to settle down.

I wasn't expecting her response. She said that she really wanted to have a kid, and that even if she walked out the door the next morning and bumped into Mister or Miss Right, she was still looking at a minimum of two years of dating and cohabitating and sussing it all out before real progress toward baby-making could start. I joked that without a man in the picture it would be even trickier, and then she said something to the effect of "Well, maybe if I find myself in a serious relationship with a woman you'd consider making a donation to us."

My response was, "Only if I get to sleep with both of you," which shows how seriously I took it.

I didn't think about it again until the next time she brought it up, and then the next time and the next time. She became more and more persistent, in a way that made me realize she was very serious, but also pushed me away. The relationship she wanted had not materialized, her clock was ticking, and she had made up her mind. I was sensitive to this, but ambivalent and feeling like the whole thing was pretty far-fetched.

After a few months, I began to consider it. I felt she had so much to give to a child, and I wanted to help her. But I still felt there needed to be a serious discussion about what my role would be in the rearing of this child. I did not want a kid, or part of a kid. But once Sarah made it very clear to me that the only thing she expected from me was sperm, the idea started to gain momentum. Ultimately, when I look back on it now, it was very simple. I had an opportunity to help someone, and I felt I had to take it.

I talked to only one person, other than Sarah, about my decision. My friend Marcus is coldly rational, brutally honest, and extremely loyal. His position was that in terms of responsibilities, covering my own ass with disclaimers and caveats was only part of the equation. Having absolute trust in Sarah's ability to be a good parent was even more important, because even if I never laid eyes on the child once it was born, I would still bear responsibility for bringing it into this world.

I was still concerned that I would somehow be saddled with the responsibility of raising a child at a time in my life when I didn't want one. But once the cold hard fact that I would *not* be involved in the raising of this kid was established, that this was a gift I was giving Sarah, that this was about her and her child and not me, the only concerns left were ones of conscience. Could I trust Sarah to be a good mother? I could. She is tough and sweet and firm and loving and I knew that she would love the hell out of her baby, and never let it down.

That said, we came up with an agreement that absolved me of any responsibilities, emotional or financial, for the raising of the child. I am not on the birth certificate. In the event of Sarah's death, custody goes to her mother. I was firm about my position, though Sarah left openings for me to change things in the future. I think she definitely would have welcomed my playing a larger role, but I had to be honest with her, and I told her over and over again where I stood because I wanted total clarity. This was not a "wait and see" decision; considering the stakes, I wanted to make sure there was no ambiguity.

Working on the agreement was a challenge. It's all very abstract when you don't have an actual child, and at the time there were surprisingly few resources for charting a course like ours. Most attorneys had no idea where to start. So we ended up winging it. The process was comical—and emblematic of the moment. We were two people with zero legal training trying to come up with an official-sounding contract regarding an issue with almost no legal precedent.

Sarah roughed out the bulk of it based on our many conversations, and to her credit, it reflected my needs pretty well. She'd e-mail me a draft; I'd make some edits and send it back. The whole process was smooth, and it contributed to my feelings of detachment. Once you've gone through all of the worst-case scenarios on paper—death, debilitation, and abandonment—it's hard to remember that you're talking about a person-to-be. And since all of these scenarios ended with me out of the picture, the detachment was reinforced. At that point I really did start feeling like a sperm-delivery device. Which was exactly what I wanted.

Ultimately, we finished the agreement and had an attorney look it over. Now we each have a document tucked away in a folder somewhere that may or may not be binding.

There were so many unknowns, and there still are. We made the agreement as comprehensive as we could, while keeping in mind that things would come up that we hadn't considered. In short, things might be weird sometimes, but never so weird that it supersedes the fundamental goodness of this child's existence. What's a little weirdness compared to a happy, healthy mom and child?

At one point, an attorney suggested I be paid financial compensation for my end of the deal, if only to make the arrangement more of a "transaction" and less of an emotional relationship. I didn't want money, but Sarah kept trying to pay me—first it was $1,000, then it was $100, and in the end she showed up at my house with a carload of potted shrubs for my then-barren yard.

We conceived the old-fashioned way. Sarah mapped out a number of optimal dates, based on her cycle. She was adamant about making the most of each of those dates and when one fell on a Sunday that was both a long workday *and* my birthday, I pleaded with her to get out of it. I made my case to her over the phone but she wasn't having it, and when I pulled up to my apartment thirty minutes later she was sitting on the front steps.

We went inside, up the stairs to the bedroom, and in twenty minutes we were done. She insisted on keeping her legs in the air for a good fifteen minutes after each attempt (letting gravity do its part), so when a friend showed up ten minutes later I pretended nothing was going on. I kept trying to get us out of the apartment but he insisted on one, then two, then three rounds of Wild Turkey shots before we left. Sarah listened to the whole thing from upstairs and had to muffle her laughs with a pillow. Ten days later she was officially pregnant.

Aside from actually impregnating her, I didn't have an active role in the pregnancy. I got more information, sooner, about all of the tests and developments and kicks, and I probably had a better window into her emotional state than I would have had otherwise. But while I was perfectly aware that the baby growing inside her was "mine," I wasn't torn up about it. I had made a decision about how I was going to feel—detached, but in a warm way—and that's how I felt.

I didn't tell any of my friends or family, except Marcus, until Sarah was actually pregnant, and I think her mother was the only person in her life who knew what she was up to. Our feeling was that a decision had been made, with no small amount of consideration and discussion, and opening it up for the input of others, especially before she was actually pregnant, was going to create interference. I also think that after all of the back and forth we just didn't want anyone trying to talk us out of it.

I told my mom first. She was surprised but completely accepted it in her warm Southern way. I think that once she knew that Sarah was open to her meeting and having a relationship with her and the child, she was excited and happy, just as a potential grandmother would be. Sarah's attitude was,

"As long as she doesn't try to tell me how to raise this kid, she can love the baby all she wants. The more love the better." So while I was setting a bunch of boundaries and limits on responsibilities, my mom was shopping for baby clothes.

It gave me pause at first. I felt my position might be undermined a bit by my mother's enthusiasm. But she and Sarah hit it off on their own terms. They like each other, and just as I expect my wishes as an individual to be respected, I have to respect theirs. If I thought my mom misunderstood my role, and wanted to assume greater responsibility than she has, I'd be worried. But as far as I can tell, she gets it.

We told friends and the rest of my family soon after. People were very supportive for the most part. One explanation was generally all it took for people to figure it out. If anyone disapproved or was upset about it, they didn't show it. I told my dad, stepmom, and other members of the family before a big dinner. They were all sitting on the couch and I stood up and said that I had something big to share with them. My dad turned white and grabbed my stepmom's knee. I think he thought I was going to announce that I was gay.

Of course a few people expected or wanted me to feel differently. Some actually told me either what I should feel or what I would feel, which bothered me. They said things like, "Oh, but once that child is born you'll want to be much more involved," or "How could you not want to play a part in his or her upbringing?" There was lots of projection from others, and a fair amount of defensiveness from me. I was hyperaware of the fact that others were judging me based on my attitude. I tried not to get worked up, and reminded myself I had made the right decision based on who I am and how I felt. Why bullshit myself?

I was not at the birth. Had I wanted to, I could have been. But I didn't. I am a donor, not a father, and I made it clear from the beginning that playing any fatherly role would only muddle the issue. No reason to start then, plus Sarah had a midwife, two doulas, her mother, sister, two friends, and a birthing tub. Even if I had wanted to be there they probably would have kicked me out! She pushed for the better part of three days, and in the end went to Kaiser and got a C-section.

I went to the hospital the next day with a mutual friend. I felt the way I would have if any one of my close friends had a child. I was happy that the baby, whom Sarah named Jake, was healthy. I was happy that Sarah had survived the birth, and relieved that that stage was over. But I was not overcome by a torrent of parental emotion. My feelings didn't suddenly change. Some people have a hard time believing or understanding that. But it is what it is. I felt good—for Sarah and her baby. It was about them, not me.

I see Jake roughly once every few months, though there is no set schedule. Birthdays and holidays, annual visits by my mom from Georgia—all of these occasions mean we hang out. The visits with my mom are probably the most intimate. Usually it's just Mom, Sarah, Jake, and me, hanging out in a park, talking and playing. The relationship that Sarah and my mom have is remarkably easy and free of tension. They're genuinely fond of each other and I think my mom, having raised my sister and me on her own, really appreciates what Sarah is going through. She knows it's not easy being a single mom, and that Sarah is doing an amazing job.

I didn't have a steady girlfriend during the discussion and conception periods, or for most of the pregnancy, but my current girlfriend, Melissa, also has a great relationship with Sarah and Jake. No tension, no awkwardness, just an immediate comfort level that is a testament to everyone's fundamental goodness. Jake seems to be very fond of Melissa in particular, and I think this is a reflection not just of Melissa's likability but also of Sarah's warmth toward her. Kids respond to cues from their parents.

I told Melissa early on, well before we were getting serious. She looked a little wide-eyed at first, like she was being let in on a secret. But once I broke it down she was surprisingly accepting and understanding. It may be unusual, but it's not that complicated. And it was clear to her that it was a well thought out, very deliberate act between two consenting adults. There was none of the shame or residual anger often attached to parents who part ways.

If something were to change and I found myself fathering a child in a more traditional way, I would look forward to him or her having a special friendship with Jake. It's hard to describe that kind of relationship in a word—*fraternal* or *familial* just doesn't cut it. I would just want them to know and love each other. Sarah and I decided from the beginning that there would be no secrets, namely between her and me and Jake, but I think that principle extends into the world around us, and our different relationships. Secrets turn into lies and lies can turn poisonous. Any short-term awkwardness that might result from honesty and openness is so much easier on everyone than the effects of a long-held secret.

At this point it's still pretty early for Jake to be asking any really penetrating questions, but Sarah's approach has been to answer questions when they're asked. Jake knows that I am his "father," but at age three I don't think that he has a real understanding of what that word means. He knows that some kids have "fathers" who are big parts of their lives, but he also knows other kids who have two moms or no father at all. So for the time being, my presence or lack of it is probably just one small and confusing part of a big confusing world. As he gets smart enough to ask more questions, he'll get more answers.

I would not do it again. Not because I regret it, but rather because once is enough. Sarah actually asked me a year ago if I'd consider donating again so that she could have a second child. It initially struck me as preposterous, though I can understand why she would (a) want Jake to have a sibling and (b) want to do it sooner rather than later. But those reasons aren't enough to change my mind. I am content, happy—relieved even—with the way things have turned out, and I can handle the emotional effects.

A balance exists, between my expectations and Sarah's, as well as those of all of our friends and family. And while there may be occasional minor bumps in the road, I think that the overall situation is very stable and secure and bodes well for Jake's future. And while adding another child to the mix is not in itself a bad thing, I think that it needs to happen with a true partner to Sarah, who will be there for all of them in the long run.

I don't know that our type of family will ever be the norm. The norm, for better or for worse, will probably always be a man and a woman in a relationship having a child together. Whether or not that man will stick around is another story. But I do think that relationships or arrangements like mine and Sarah's will come to be more accepted, particularly as more and more gays and lesbians have kids, through adoption or natural means. I certainly hope they become more accepted, because I think there's something fundamentally more strong and stable about a family that makes a very deliberate choice to raise a child, particularly when there are cultural and legal obstacles they know full well might get in their way. They're doing it because they really, really want to, and their children will most likely be better for it.

As acceptance grows, it also shows people that they have more choices for how to live their lives than they realize. Sarah chose to have and raise a child on her own. She was brave enough to see it as an option, and she went for it.

She was also lucky enough to get working sperm for the cost of a couple of potted plants.

9.
Two Red Lines
Susan McKinney de Ortega

A friend I haven't seen in twenty-five years found me on the Internet and wrote from Minnesota, "Would love to see your daughters. Do they look Hispanic?"

My daughters were born in Mexico to a Mexican father and me, a former Philadelphia Irish Catholic. "Do they speak English?" and "Are there decent schools down there?" are other questions I get from Americans who don't quite understand how I could have married a poor kid from the barrio and never returned to the land of opportunity. At my wedding, half of the guests finishing my mother-in-law's chicken mole were making bets about how long we would stay married. Odds were six months to a year.

In fact, Carlos and I have been married for twelve years. He is still fifteen years younger than I, but we are no longer poor. Our differences and lack of a clearly mapped future are what made my mother call a family meeting when I announced my pending wedding thirteen years ago. My siblings were summoned to Philadelphia from Washington,

D.C., Boston, and the Virgin Islands by phone. The theme: how to get Susan out of Mexico.

"She'll lead her life in poverty," my mother wailed.

"She's always liked to shock people. Maybe this is only a way to get attention," my brother John offered.

"She is thirty-four years old. She appears to be happy. I think we need to go down there and support her," my father said.

My father's gift as a basketball coach was that he was a motivator. He got stellar performances from players by believing in them and guiding them to believe in themselves. On this, he built winning teams and earned two NBA championship rings. At games and award ceremonies, I was the first on my feet, cheering louder than the rest.

Growing up surrounded by the macho world of sports, where men adjusted their jockstraps at the foul line and sank buzzer shots to win ball games, you would think I'd end up with a headlining man of some sort. A coach, an athletic director, a referee even.

Instead, I found a quiet guy who hadn't finished high school and could barely grow a mustache; who, true, spent his afternoon on the town's basketball courts, but otherwise was the farthest thing from the world I came from I could imagine. He wasn't even tall.

In 1992 I came to San Miguel de Allende in the Mexican Central highlands to work on a memoir about trying to find a place in that athletic world. Writing, I discovered I'd coasted through my youth soaking up attention from being the coach's daughter. In first grade, Sister Virgo pasted a gold star on my Peter Pan collar when the Hawks of St. Joseph's College beat Villanova. At the end of my freshman year in college, I watched the Trailblazers win the 1977 NBA Championship, and the following day rode through downtown Portland on the back of a convertible in the victory parade. In Indiana, when my father coached the Pacers, I was interviewed on the radio about what it was like to live with Jack McKinney. As a result, I'd never developed a fully formed identity of my own. Perhaps I knew I had to cross a border to do so.

The day before I left for Mexico, I posed for a picture in the alley behind the White Dog Café, where I bartended. I wore white socks, Doc Martens, and a Doris Day dress with darts under the breasts from a vintage shop on Walnut and sat on the hood of the 1985 Dodge I would leave with my roommate. My legs were folded to one side; I held one hand behind my head.

"Act your age," my mother sometimes said to me, half joking. I was thirty-four years old. If I acted my age, I would be having children.

By the end of that first Mexican summer, I'd made some friends, written some chapters, and fallen in love with the rich colors, the deep sunlight, the lime trees, the quiet cobblestone streets, the unhurried life I led in San Miguel. But my money was running out.

I walked to an English-language school one afternoon, résumé and references in hand. But the director asked me only one question: "Can you take all the afternoon classes?"

I became an English teacher.

What was it about the nineteen-year-old with a Flock of Seagulls haircut sitting in a front desk that captured me that first day? That once he took off his black sunglasses, he had nice eyes? That he saw my nervousness and smiled encouragingly? That he watched me, not suggestively like the other boys did, but with compassion, as I gamely struggled to speak enough Spanish to teach them English?

One day, walking up and down the aisles while the students worked on a verb exercise, I pointed to a beaded cross Carlos wore around his neck. "That's nice," I said, then felt foolish.

Leaving the school building in the afternoon, I heard footsteps behind me. When I turned, Carlos lifted the cross from his neck and placed it over my head. I tried to picture a guy in Philly giving me a simple gift and walking away, but could only imagine the usual—conversations in a bar with all threads leading back to the real topic: whether I would go home with him that night. I walked from the school grounds, feeling the ghost of Carlos's hands where they'd floated past my head and lightly touched my shoulders.

Carlos waited after classes during those first weeks and casually mentioned on three occasions that we should go to Laberintos, a San Miguel disco, before I accepted. I was the teacher, after all. And he was nineteen. And gorgeous. I brought a friend along so it wouldn't be a date.

By the end of the evening, Carlos and I were kissing under the glittery disco ball, and through the next year we were inseparable, although we kept our distance on school grounds.

Teaching a few classes a week for five dollars an hour didn't leave me much to live on. Eventually I moved out of my small apartment and into Carlos's house, where we shared his childhood bed in a room occupied by us and his brother and sister. This was normal for Carlos's family, as, besides the kitchen, the house had only two rooms. I had to adjust, however, to sleeping in my clothes like they did, changing in the shower room, and having the naked overhead lightbulb turned on whenever anyone entered the room, no matter how late at night.

The house sat on a tiny plot of land on the edge of town. It had no telephone or hot water and about ten people living in it, including the ex-girlfriend of one of Carlos's brothers and their two children. Plus, a cousin from León had left her no-good husband and come with four children to live in the house. On top of that, a neighbor had given Carlos's mother a litter of piglets, which she put in the home's floor-to-ceiling bird hutch.

I was absorbed into the family without much fuss. I concluded it was because we caused the least amount of problems. I had a job, Carlos went to school, and we had no extra-relationship children.

Probably hardest for me to get used to was how the broom would begin to scritch the floor of the room over Carlos's bed every morning at seven. It scolded me, "Get up, get up, get up." All the other women of the house were already out of bed, sweeping, mopping, mashing frijoles, trudging to a neighbor's house to buy fresh *atole*, a thick corn drink I couldn't stomach. Nobody roused me out of bed, and, like the men, I slept as late as I pleased. What was my place? I wanted to bond with the women but was furious with their servitude. So I stayed in bed, eyes wide open from seven a.m. on, poking my boyfriend so he could wake up and feel the injustice too.

As the blush of new love deepened, I realized I had gotten myself into a life where good times meant a meal with meat. Here's a whole group of people living the simple life. Why can't I? I asked myself. Because you weren't born into this, and there is nothing wrong with having hot showers and a washing machine, I answered. Perhaps most daunting was the lack of privacy. To find it, I climbed to the roof, sat under the fluttering laundry, and read.

What am I doing here? I asked myself daily. I'm barely earning enough to live, and my boyfriend hasn't finished high school. I'm supposed to be a person with a job, deadlines, a cup of coffee, a newspaper, I told myself. And a partner with a future.

Oh, yeah? According to whom? the devil on my left shoulder argued.

I imagined packing my things and going back to Philadelphia. Back to bartending and getting home at three a.m. Getting out of the cab and stabbing looks into every dark corner of my South Philly street to let attackers know they would not catch me off guard. Going to parties in giant warehouse lofts, paying a cover at the door so the artist friends who lived there could have their heat turned back on. Sitting in my room alone in the winter chill, trying to write. It made me shudder.

I tried to imagine myself married to a nice Philadelphia lawyer who lived for Saturday football games on a big-screen

TV in a big house, but only saw someone else next to that man. I could not picture myself.

So I stayed. I learned to make Carlos's mother's salsas. I helped her cut toenails off the chicken feet she would fry and sell to neighborhood children. I paid the ex-girlfriend to hand-wash my clothes, and I walked into town, creating my own private space on the streets. Carlos and I watched basketball games in the park, and when he talked about dropping out of school I encouraged him to finish.

The nagging thoughts I had about returning to my respectable life were surrendered one day in April 1994 when I sat on the side of a bathtub and watched double lines appear on a pregnancy test strip. Two red lines pointing my life in a new direction.

Early on our wedding day, my mother-in-law-to-be, Carmen, opened nuts with a hammer in her kitchen, preparing chicken mole for the reception, and told me how she had gotten married. There had been a government campaign on the radio to get people living together to marry, she said. She worked, cleaning and cooking in the home of a rich Mexican woman who said, "*Ándale*, Doña Carmen. Why don't you take the day off and get married?"

"So I thought, why not?" Carmen told me. "I went home to Silvano and said, '*Vámonos, viejo,*' and we went down to the *registro* and a judge married us."

She had wiped her hands on her T-shirt, changed her shoes, taken the bus to the *centro* with her man, and signed some papers. Then they'd come home, where she'd left a pot of *frijoles* on a low boil, and she'd sent Carlos's sister Dora up the street for fresh tortillas.

"How long ago was that?" I'd asked.

"Carlos was in *secundaria*. Eh, four or five years ago."

My parents had married at ages twenty-one and twenty-two, when my father was home in Chester, Pennsylvania, from Army Reserve duty. The wedding was during the Christmas season. The bridesmaids wore deep green and the halls were decked with boughs of holly.

Carlos and I planned a small ceremony, something between the styles of our parents'. We contracted a justice of the peace. A friend lent her spacious garden, populated with fruit trees.

My family flew in from east and west. Our wedding day was a Monday. My father paced in the garden.

"'On time' has a different meaning in Mexico," I soothed. "The judge will come."

Upstairs, I kept watch at the window. Dora, my soon-to-be sister-in-law, teetered through the gate on high heels, carrying a huge pot. She stood, looking around, until my father appeared and took the pot from her. My friend Betsy arranged white gladiolas in a ceramic pot.

Cha-Cha, a translator, came upstairs holding a rum and Coke. "*Muchachas*, the judge arrived at my wedding at midnight. All the guests were sloshed by then. The judge was tanked. My husband says he's not sure we got married."

"Don't let my father hear you say that."

Below, guests continued to arrive. There was my boss at a company that imported medical equipment—a white Mexican who had whispered to my sister how stunned he was that I, a person with education, could have become engaged to someone so *morenito*, so low-class.

In the garden, Carmen arrived, followed by Silvano, tugging a borrowed sports coat around him.

"*Ven conmigo*," I said to my future in-laws. I led Carmen and Silvano to where my mother stood in a moss green garden party dress. "Mom," I said. "This is Carlos's mother, Carmen."

"Oh," my mother said with warmth, lowering her wineglass to a stone tree border. Unable to speak each other's language, the two mothers hugged. Then the judge arrived.

I scurried back to the house to make my entrance on the garden path.

My father, dressed in a gray summer wool suit, held out his arm and flashed me a go-get-'em smile.

Smiling faces lined the flagstone path, my mother with tears in the corners of her eyes, my friends craning to see me. I knew some of them still whispered that Carlos was too young, unformed, prospectless for me. I marched on. I knew our life would not be easy. I also knew I had found genuine love and this was my path.

My parents managed to get through the wedding with some degree of satisfaction and even joy. Carlos and I went back to his parents' house, where we'd built a small apartment, and where we brought Carla Xochítl when she was born.

Carla, a few days old, lay on the bed next to me one day as I leafed through an American women's magazine that addressed new mothers. "You can't get enough sleep and don't have time to buy groceries or pick up the house. Plus there's that work deadline you'll never get to with your new-born demanding all your time!" it screeched. That's not me, I thought calmly, as my mother-in-law entered the room with homemade chicken soup on a tray. The benefits of living with the family, I thought sleepily. That's what I should write about.

But as much as my in-laws helped me through new motherhood, I knew I had to leave the overcrowded house, to allow my husband to grow up, to establish our own bicultural family, and to honor the traditions of both heritages.

After the birth of our second child, I found us a ninety-dollar-a-month apartment, and with baby Sean Paula in my arms and Carla toddling at our feet, we moved downtown. The privacy was achingly beautiful.

The first thing I did was make the rule that everyone sit at the table together to eat. "Why?" whined Carlos, Carla, and Sean. Carla took her plate, stomped to the patio steps outside, and began eating as she'd always done in my mother-in-law's house. I made myself immune to her screams of protest as I brought her back to the table.

Perhaps the hardest part of being in our marriage is that Carlos grew up with little structure, and I firmly believe in it. I will tell you that eleven years after we had that three-day struggle over how to eat a meal, we sit down together every single night now, and look forward to it. And that I win most of our how-to-be-a-family discussions, because my father's disciplined nature was passed firmly to me, and I believe that our way is good. I believe that regular bedtimes and mandatory school attendance and expectations that children finish their homework arm kids with tools for life. And because Carlos can see that his routineless upbringing, in which nobody insisted he go to school or come home at night, has left him unprepared for modern life. Now that he is in college, and struggling to form study habits, he backs up my rules in a more genuine way than ever. Many nights the two girls study with their father at the dining table. Sometimes it chokes me up.

I try to make room for the take-every-day-as-it-comes Mexican outlook in our lives, because it helps keep one from early heart attacks. I also see that its flip side is a staggering inertia. My father-in-law is a construction *maestro*, mixing cement and laying brick to build San Miguel's houses. Many *albañiles*, once they earn enough money for frijoles, tortillas, and tequila, will take a day off. My father-in-law, with his relaxed attitude about work, will never grasp his chest and keel over. He will also never do major repairs on his own house or take his family on a vacation—there is never any extra money.

Carlos and I don't try too hard to steer our children, now ages thirteen and eleven, away from inertia and toward hard work and savings. We let them look around. At the Ortegas' house, my mother-in-law spends the day at an outdoor gas cook stove, making and serving meals to various extended family members as they drop in. First comes Silvano, their grandfather, on his lunch break, his hands still dusty from a construction job. Next, their twenty-year-old cousin and his pregnant wife. Then their uncle, Carlos's brother Hector, after a day of teaching gym classes in San Miguel schools. In wanders the señora from down the *callejón* who never has enough cash or food. Plates of beef and potatoes in *chile pasilla* sauce are passed around, along with jokes. Carla and Sean take a plate and sit on a step or a rock or a plastic chair with their food. They enjoy the chatter and the relaxed afternoon, which might go on for hours. They see the two or three bent forks, the cracked plates, the crumbling-down house. They don't ask for napkins because there aren't any.

At my parents' house in Naples, Florida, at Christmas this year, we sat twenty-one people at two long tables lit with tapered candles. A tall tree trimmed in ornaments and white lights blazed behind us. My father's trophies sat in the back room. We said prayers, poured wine, oohed over the roast, kept our elbows off the table. One of the successes of our marriage is how our girls float effortlessly between the two homes, the two worlds.

The girls look Mexican but not quite, I told my Minnesota friend Mina. Carlos is dark brown with midnight-black hair, and I am so fair I've had several precancerous spots removed from my face. The girls are two beautiful shades of *café con leche*.

"The way kids in the States are overscheduled is nuts," Mina wrote. "What do your girls do?"

They go to a sweet little Montessori school and they ride horses, I tell Mina. I will go to the poorhouse to keep them in both.

"Are they truly bilingual?" texts Mina, whose mother is from Spain.

My girls speak both languages perfectly, something they thought every kid did until they entered grade school and realized most of their peers spoke only Spanish. What they are lacking, I write, was a good English class. Literature, poetry, writing—the kind of English the nuns taught me. The classes in their school are for children learning English as a second language. So, guess what else I'm doing besides writing and running our family business, the spa I opened with Carlos last year, Mina? You got it. Teaching English.

The next worry is where they will go to high school. Prepatoria El Pipila, where Carlos went and where nobody ever did homework and the teachers weren't paid, is not an option. Boarding school in the States is the answer for some American parents in San Miguel, but not for me. I like my kids! I want them around.

I want . . . I want . . . what I want for my kids is what I had: a large well-established high school, a swim club around the corner, a decent newspaper on the doormat, summers at the Jersey shore, a noisy gang of cousins to man baseball teams and horseshoe tournaments at family picnics.

I want them to inherit the drive and determination and shoot-for-the-stars outlook that made my father a winner. I want them to get out of bed with purpose and joy, knowing the world holds opportunities for them.

In San Miguel, my girls go to their Tío Hector's sports camp, ride with their Pony Club, compete in dressage competitions, and watch their father play basketball in the park with a gang of cousins, like in my childhood. It's not all the same, though. In their world, Corona, Guadalupe, and Rafa Márquez are patriotic words. Fireworks light up the skies about a hundred nights a year to celebrate the patron saint of a neighborhood, the cigarette sellers, a wedding. Ladies in stores tell you, if you don't have enough money, to come back and pay tomorrow. My girls can count on finding their *abuelita* next to her stove, their aunts, uncles, and cousins gathering at her table any afternoon they care to stop by. Which brings me to another wish: I want my girls to feel fully entitled to linger for hours over a home-cooked meal. There is both security and challenge to their lives, which is what I truly want, after all.

Silvano, between construction jobs, is working on the house we've started with seed money from my parents. It's a Mexican-style project. When we have extra money, we buy another load of bricks. We have a few rooms, some rebar sticking out here and there, stairs to the unfinished second floor, no debt. Before we finished a bedroom for the girls, we slept all together in one room. It was normal for my kids, out of necessity for me, shocking to American friends.

I wonder if some day being bicultural will have some meaning to the girls. Perhaps, if they go to the States for college. Will they feel American enough to not be foreign students? Will they feel their Mexicanness when they are away from Mexico?

What I understand after all these years of living in Mexico is that my life is not quite the escapist paradise some Americans fantasize it to be, nor is it the directionless poverty road we faced when we started. It is a life defined by less income than most of my American peers have, but by family bonds and a cultural richness I wouldn't trade for a dozen big houses.

We celebrate Halloween and Día de los Muertos, Christmas and Día de los Santos Reyes. We have *posadas* and *piñatas*, ice cream, cake, and iPods. Despite all wedding bets, Carlos and I are still in this life together, teaching each other alternately to succeed and relax, and above all, to enjoy the gifts we were given.

10.
My First Husband Liza Monroy

"I don't know how to tell you this," said Razi. "So I'm just going to say it. I have to go home."

At first I didn't understand what he meant. Razi, my gay best friend, lived six blocks away from me in West Hollywood, California. He'd come over to my apartment that sunny, late October afternoon for a *Sex and the City* marathon. It had been a year since we graduated from the Boston film school where we'd met and become inseparable.

"You forgot something?" I asked.

"Not home to Havenhurst Drive, sweetie," he said. "*Home* home."

"What?" I asked. "Why?"

First I was shocked by Razi's admission, and then I was scared. He was from a predominantly Muslim country, and this was only a month after September 11th. Was he being deported?

"My student visa is expiring," Razi continued. "No company wants to sponsor me for a work visa because entry-level entertainment jobs require no special skill."

It suddenly made sense. There were plenty of U.S. citizens

eager to have staplers tossed at them by manic studio executives for twenty thousand dollars a year. Razi had a window to turn his F-1 visa into an H1B by getting hired by a company willing to sponsor him. I knew this because visas had played a prominent role in my life. My mother had started her diplomatic career in the visa section of a U.S. consulate in Mexico. My first job in high school had been in the visa section of the embassy in Mexico City, where my mother was Chief of Citizen Services. I did data entry and laminated the visas, studying each person's face and name and silently wishing them a better life.

I feared for Razi's future. Our plan had been to find film-industry jobs in Los Angeles. So far, I had freelanced as a production assistant on a Spike Jonze movie and Razi had an internship at a big studio. If he were sent back to his country, he could never fulfill his dream of becoming a screenwriter and film producer. Worse yet, he would have to go back to hiding his sexual orientation from his family and his community. He was growing increasingly desperate with each passing day.

"I know that if I go back I'll become one of those married men with children who look for boys online or street corners," he said. "I'll end up not living my life."

Where Razi was from, gay sex was considered criminal behavior. I couldn't let him go back to that.

And then one night I found myself saying, "I'd rather marry you than see you sent home."

And then Razi said, "Don't joke around about that, sweetie, I might take you up on it."

Was it a joke? I was unsure.

"Maybe I *am* serious," I said, simultaneously thinking:

What am I doing? It couldn't really come down to that—could it? Now that it was out there, I couldn't take it back. But I was sure Razi would land a job soon enough and this marriage talk would be forgotten as quickly as it had come up.

"Thank you, sweetie." He smiled sincerely. "I'll consider it an absolute last resort."

I hadn't premeditated a marriage proposal. It just dropped out of my mouth, surprising me as much as it did Razi.

I had never had childhood fantasies of beaded white dresses and tossing a bouquet. After witnessing the decline of my parents' marriage when I was six years old, I decided I would never marry at all—the whole business seemed like too much trouble. When it came to my own romantic life, I had a habit of always wanting the wrong men. In L.A., I fell in love with a commitment-phobic music video director who was ten years my senior. After a brief fling, I spent many heartbreaking months pursuing him. I wished my relationships could be as uncomplicated as the unconditional, non-sexual love that I had with Razi.

I thought I would keep my promise to Razi if it came to that, but I hoped and prayed he'd find a job. A fake marriage to my gay best friend sounded like a funny romantic comedy premise, but actually going through with it was another matter. If the INS did not believe we were in a real marriage, he could face deportation and I might be jailed. I spent the successive weeks grilling Razi about every job interview. He would look at the ground, eyes downcast, and shake his head. I e-mailed all my work leads, desperately searching for someone to help him so we wouldn't have to resort to my life-altering plan.

But two months passed, and nothing changed. As his visa's expiration date approached and Razi began talking about booking his flight home, I knew what I had to do. I cared about him too much. I had to keep my word.

We were sitting outdoors one balmy autumn evening at the Abbey, our favorite West Hollywood gay bar. Razi shared the story of his latest interview. As usual, it had ended abruptly when he brought up the visa factor.

"That's enough," I said, leaping onto my knees in a purposefully exaggerated comical gesture. "Consider us officially engaged."

I moved into his apartment the next day. I never imagined that, like my mother, I would tie the knot at the age of twenty-two—and that my marriage would involve lying to her, just as she had lied to my grandparents when she married my father.

When my mother was twenty-two, she and her MGB convertible traveled by boat from New York to teach English in Florence. One evening, she noticed the tall, handsome maitre d' in the ship's restaurant. They felt an instant connection and decided to get married as soon as the boat docked. For this, my mother needed her birth certificate. She asked her parents to send it to Genoa, saying she'd met a wealthy Italian baron. They would never have sent it over had they known he actually came from a family of farmers. After the wedding, they settled in Seattle.

Eleven years later, in 1985, I was five years old and the strains on their marriage were showing. My father drank heavily after his shifts waiting tables at an Italian restaurant. In a desire for some way out, my mother joined the U.S.

Foreign Service and transferred to Mexico, taking me with her. My parents divorced and my father rented a studio near downtown Seattle. He worked at the same Italian restaurant until, during my senior year of high school, he disappeared. I would call his number and let it ring ten, twelve, fifteen times before softly placing the phone back in the receiver. I'm sure that if he hadn't met my mother, my father would have married a provincial Italian girl and settled in his hometown. When my efforts to locate him turned up empty, I made myself believe that was where he'd gone.

Razi and I got together at a Starbucks on Sunset to finalize the last-minute plans he'd cobbled together—our wedding plans were made entirely through the Las Vegas chapel's online reservation system. It was my lunch break from the bad independent film I was working on as an assistant and my mind was foggy from late hours, too much caffeine, and not enough food. It was another hot November day in Los Angeles, with cars going by on the boulevard outside. Palm fronds rustled in the warm Santa Ana winds.

We hugged hello and Razi ran down the itinerary. We would be married by a man in an Elvis costume, and Razi's dad had sent us a thousand dollars each for gambling as a wedding present. I said everything sounded like so much fun, but there was no hiding the trepidation buried beneath my sunny exterior.

"Are you feeling ready, sweetie?" he asked.

"Ready as I'll ever be," I joked. The day before the wedding, reality had sunk in.

"I just hope you don't have regrets," he said. "What if you meet someone sooner than you expect?"

"It's clear that a normal marriage wouldn't ever work for me. So I'm putting my ability to marry toward a worthy cause—you. Besides, the right guy is *so* going to get what this is about," I said.

I acted calm for Razi, but I was terrified: Could it all blow up in my face, ending with Razi being deported and my mother disowning me? Would we really pull it off, or were we just two clueless kids in way over our heads? My mother's job was to keep people like Razi and me from getting away with this—I couldn't even imagine her reaction.

Yet I felt, given my life growing up, never really having the chance to get to know my dad, that my mother might understand my personal reasons for choosing to marry Razi, if she tried. I had always feared ending up divorced, carrying the divorcée label like an embarrassingly bad designer knockoff purse, of failing in the only way I was desperate to succeed. I realized that marrying Razi presented me with the perfect opportunity to cement my future as a divorcée, draining the meaning out of the label. When Razi and I split, it would be a happy event. He would become a citizen of a country where he would be free to love whomever he chose.

"I'm in love, I'm all shook up," the fake Elvis sang as Razi and I danced our way down the aisle. Elvis wore a bad wig and a shiny red fake silk button-down. He gyrated his hips, a painful exaggeration of the original King's moves.

"I think the minister's gay," Razi whispered, gesturing at the older man.

"Act straighter," I teased.

Razi adjusted his tie and puffed up his chest like a football player and we both laughed.

As we danced to the ridiculous music in the shanty building on the Vegas Strip, my nervousness evaporated. I felt happy and free for the first time in a year.

"Do you promise to polish each other's blue suede shoes?" Elvis asked.

"I do," I said.

"Do you promise to walk each other's hound dogs?"

"Of course," Razi replied.

"I'm more of a cat person," I said, "but sure."

A few months later, my mother arrived in L.A. for a visit. We made dinner plans, and she asked me to bring that roommate of mine she'd always been so fond of—Razi. In the crowded Chaya Brasserie, a posh Asian-fusion restaurant, my mother was her usual chipper, extroverted self, asking Razi about his career goals. I fiddled with my shrimp as he answered her questions about his job hunt.

When Razi got up and went to the bathroom, my mother leaned over the table and gave me a concerned look. "How is Razi staying in the country?" she asked. "He must be illegal now; his student visa would have expired months ago."

"Mom, I have no idea," I said, resisting the lump rising in my throat. I was terrified.

"If he *is* illegal, no one is going to hire him. Could he have found an American and gotten married?"

"No," I said, trying to remain composed. "I don't think so. If he had I would have known about it."

"Well, that's certainly odd. Maybe I'll look up his status in the system at work." She picked up a menu off the table as Razi sat back down. "What sounds good for dessert?"

My mother had originally chosen her line of work because she wanted to travel and live around the world, but along the way, she'd become invested in the job. She loved sleuthing and solving mysteries, figuring out which visa candidates were lying about their reasons for traveling to the United States and planning to stay in the country illegally.

From then on, I inhaled sharply every time she called, each time terrified she had looked Razi up in her computer and uncovered the truth. But she never mentioned it again and eventually I figured she'd forgotten about her questions.

Meanwhile, Razi and I grew closer as roommates in his spacious, ground-floor West Hollywood apartment. Neither of us had any desire to be lovers, but we were more than best friends. Our marriage was eccentric, but it worked better than any situation I'd had with a real boyfriend—there wasn't any jealousy or possessiveness and I wouldn't feel neglected if Razi wanted to go out with his friends instead of staying in with me. We relied on each other but there wasn't that feeling of overwhelming emotional need I was prone to in love relationships.

But the challenges of family life came along with our pairing too.

One night Razi cooked me his spaghetti marinara for dinner. I'd finished the dishes and was watching *The Sopranos* when he began to yell—the opening strains of our first fight.

"Who taught you how to do dishes?" he snapped. "There are still bits of food stuck to these! It's disgusting! I always have to do everything around here myself."

I ran over and inspected the plates. "No, they're clean," I argued. "You're so compulsive about the littlest things. Why don't you go out and get a job?"

"If I knew you were going to nag me like a real wife, I'd have gone home and gotten beheaded."

Sometimes the seriousness of our circumstances would hit me all at once. Arguments about dirty dishes weren't ever really about dirty dishes. Whether I liked it or not, I held the upper hand in our relationship because his ability to stay in the country depended on me. I didn't think about it at the time, but I let Razi pay most of the household bills and buy our groceries with the monthly allowance his father sent him, and do the vast majority of domestic chores. He was the perfect husband. He generally wouldn't say anything about feeling resentful, but at times he must have been. He knew I'd done him a tremendous favor by marrying him, but that alone couldn't quell the accompanying subsurface tensions and minor complications that inevitably arose in such a close relationship.

Razi started waiting tables and selling spa packages to Botoxed housewives on Rodeo Drive, and I wondered why he'd stopped looking for film-industry jobs as soon as he finally had the opportunity to get one. I knew that the consistent rejections he'd faced while seeking visa sponsorship had tired him, but he didn't need to worry about that anymore. Half the reason I married him was so he could get a job. I had faith in Razi's ambitions, but now I worried he might not follow through on them, just as my father had dreamed of opening his own restaurant yet never took any action. Anxious about Razi's professional stagnation and frustrated by my own sporadic freelance gigs, I began interviewing for steady jobs, steady work, steadiness. Eventually I was hired as an assistant at a talent and literary agency.

At work, I developed a crush on a bookishly handsome literary department assistant. I typed his name into Yahoo, the Google before Google, like any good aspiring writer conducting her research. Usually I found nothing—maybe that a guy I was interested in had been a high school football champion, or perhaps he'd written for a newspaper or won statewide debate awards. Not in this case. The first thing that came up was an LAPD Web page. I found out he had been wanted for stealing hundreds of thousands of dollars' worth of rare books. I was fascinated—the object of my crush was a rogue book thief disguised as a mild-mannered glorified secretary. I imagined the two of us as soul mates, me providing a West Hollywood Underground Railroad for gay immigrants, him piling his shelves high with masterfully swiped first-edition copies of *Ulysses* and *Moby-Dick*. He was a literary James Bond, I a one-woman asylum-granter. I called the detective listed on the website. I had no gains of turning him in, but I craved more details about his crimes.

"The detective's not in right now," said the woman who answered and asked what my call was regarding. "Whom may I tell him called?"

I panicked. I hadn't thought of a pseudonym and I couldn't leave my real name in case it somehow got back to the perpetrator.

"Razi Adivar," I blurted. I gave our home number. I didn't think twice about it.

Within hours, Razi called me at work, infuriated.

"How could you do this to me?" he demanded. "Do you have any idea what a huge panic attack I had when a detective from the LAPD called our house looking for me? He left a message on the machine! It said, this is such-and-such officer from the LAPD calling for Razi Adivar. Did you think this was some kind of joke?"

Razi had thought he was going to be arrested because somehow we'd been found out. After hyperventilating and smoking half a pack of cigarettes, he called our immigration lawyer and she told him the INS didn't work through police departments, so Razi called the detective back to figure out what was going on.

"I finally put two and two together when they said the Razi Adivar who called was a woman," he said. "Turns out your book thief already did his time. One of that detective's favorite cases, apparently."

"I'm so sorry about this," I said, feeling awful.

"I hope you're satisfied," he said. "I can't wait until we don't have to do this anymore."

"Raz, please don't say that." His words stung.

"I love you, sweetie, but I don't think I could have married a crazier person."

Tired of Los Angeles, fruitless when it came to book thieves, jobs, and romances alike, Razi and I moved to New York City for a fresh start. I'd decided that working in the entertainment industry was way too frustrating. Razi was ambivalent about the move; he wouldn't have gone if it weren't for me, yet he, too, admitted to having grown tired of Los Angeles. During our adventures in apartment hunting, our broker asked us if we needed a second bedroom because we were planning on a baby. We smiled and said of course. She offered us the lease on a charming two-bedroom on the Lower East Side right away. As a married couple, she said, we were highly desirable candidates.

The real estate agent wasn't the only person who thought children had a place in our future. The first visitor in our new home was Razi's father, Mohammad, a prominent businessman in the Middle East who hoped that Razi and I would fall in love during the process. I am certain that Mohammad would normally hate the idea of his firstborn only son marrying a Jewish American girl, but he was deeply in denial of Razi's sexual orientation. Razi had told his father repeatedly we were only good friends, but Mohammad would never hear it.

Though we'd only just finished decorating the new flat, Razi and I spent hours doing what he affectionately called "de-gaying" the apartment, tearing down *Absolutely Fabulous* posters and photos of Razi with his more effeminate-looking friends, and hiding the refrigerator magnet that read "Nobody Knows I'm Gay." Mohammad took us to a musical and out for dinner. His version of my mother's line of questioning was, "When do you two plan to have a child?"

"We aren't," Razi said.

"Do you think by next year you'll be pregnant?" Mohammad asked me.

"You never know," I said, and shrugged.

After Mohammad left, the *Ab Fab* posters came out of the boxes, Razi went back to being himself, and a shocking coincidence of good news arrived in the mail: Razi had won the visa lottery, a program that provides visas somewhat randomly, for diversity purposes. We no longer needed to be married.

"Can you believe it? We don't have to be married anymore," he said.

"But I don't think we should get divorced," I said. "Just in case. Something could still go wrong with your paperwork."

"I like being married to you too," he said, grasping the true meaning beneath my words. Razi was right: I loved being married to him. We told each other everything, he always listened to me, offered honest opinions, and made me laugh. We were constant companions. I realized it would take a much better reason than his green card to put an end our union. With sex and physicality out of the picture but a strong relationship—mutual appreciation, love, and kinship—in place, we'd somehow invented a deviant offshoot of marriage. Despite our occasional arguments over chores and finances, it was a beautiful thing, and we even worked through the power imbalance by striking up agreements when we argued and defining what was transpiring between us. Razi had found a job with a movie-subtitling company and agreed to pay our bills and most of the rent as long as I stepped up in the household chores department, and we each made good on our word.

Razi and I lived together for another year, and I often

forgot that the two of us were even married. We each dated, worked, and partied like the young twentysomethings we were. The one yearly reminder of our nuptials was tax time. Razi and I filed jointly, which had its benefits.

Until my mother and I decided it was a good idea to invest in real estate and buy an apartment in New York. I had finally found a stable job at a literacy agency and it seemed like the right time.

"The co-op board needs our tax returns," she announced one night over the phone.

"Okay, I'll get those together and fax them to you for the package."

I'd forgotten Razi's name was on them until page five had run through the fax machine. I was officially an idiot. Or was it more like Freud said—there are no accidents?

The phone rang. My stomach sank. I knew I couldn't avoid what was coming. "*You* married Razi!" my mother screamed when I answered.

"Yes, Mom, I did," I said, trying to remain calm. I couldn't lie now, even if I'd wanted to.

"How could you do this to me?" she cried. Her voice wavered over the phone. I tried my best to explain, feeling guiltier than ever before for hurting my mother this way, for making her cry.

"It's not something I did to *you*. I did it for him. And for me."

"But why?" she sobbed.

"Because I need him, Mom."

"What you need is to get divorced before we buy this apartment," she said.

"I know. I will." I felt terrible but also unburdened of my secret.

Razi went to divorce court to file our paperwork. We'd cited "neglect," technically, that we hadn't consummated our marriage. He said he was the only person in line at divorce court humming along to his iPod, but the day the divorce became final, as we hugged good-bye on a Chelsea street corner, we each held on a little longer, a little tighter. My mother eventually got over what I'd done and even resumed saying hello to Razi in an e-mail every now and then.

Marrying Razi wasn't a silly prank that went too far. It was love, and it didn't matter that it was nonsexual. It was real. I'd thought Razi was the one who needed me, but the reality was that he filled an empty space in my life as an only child of divorced parents. We needed each other. We had become family. We always would be.

When I married a straight man the following year, it was Razi who walked me down the aisle. And when my husband and I separated after three years together, I moved back to the Lower East Side of Manhattan, two blocks away from Razi, and right around the corner from where we had lived together. A big publisher picked up my first novel and I quit the literary agency; Razi's screenplays began placing as finalists in competitions and festivals. We've each grown, but not apart; our bond wasn't born of his need for the green card. We've been through the past four years together, sharing our lives and each other's every interest, from film and fashion to the AIDS Walk. We still meet for pedicures, cocktails with our group of friends, and long lunches, and just planned our first international adventure, a trip to South Africa. A free-spirited mutual desire to live life to its fullest has held us together through everything.

Our marriage that wasn't really a marriage ended up being so much more.

11.

Home Alone Together **Neal Pollack**

Even in our astonishingly limited social circles—Whatever
happened to friends, anyway? Didn't we once have them?—
my wife and I know families where the husband goes to
work all day and the wife (or, this being Hollywood, other
husband) stays home with the kids, seemingly without
protest. More rare, though still noticeable, are the families
where the wife pimps for Disney or busts balls for Para-
mount while the "artsy" husband captains the SS *Domestic-
ity*, only occasionally taking a week or two for a freelance
job. Also, there are families for whom domestic life is an
appendage to both partners' ten-hour workdays, whose lives
are an insane mishmash of sitter cancellations and exhausted evening dashes to Costco to buy that five-point-
harness car seat.

We are none of those families.

My wife, Regina, and I are always home, and by always, I
mean always. Yes, we work. Paying to live in this sinkhole of
a town doesn't allow for much slackitude. But we work at
home, I in the dim-lit tiled basement, she right above me, in
the only room in the house that's air-conditioned, a sunny

spot with a slanted roof and parquet floors. A couple times a month, she goes to my brother-in-law's cousin's house in the Valley to make movie-themed gift baskets for corporate hotshots. I go out of town about four weeks a year, never more than a few days consecutively. About once a month, I drive to a meeting that I'm certain will lead to the biggest career break of my life. Otherwise, I rarely leave the basement.

I'm not a househusband and Regina isn't a housewife. Neither of us particularly likes to upkeep. Though we're happy most of the time, Regina and I often say that if we could afford a cleaning service, or any kind of service, once a week or even once a month, it would help our marriage enormously. But we can't, so instead we wade through our unspecific roles, doing the best we can, trying to keep the living room free of spiderwebs. This creates mild tension, which manifests itself in conversations, usually when the kid isn't home, like:

"Why don't you do the fucking dishes?"

"Why don't *you* do the fucking dishes?"

"Because I don't fucking want to, that's why. So can you tell me why the kitchen floor is such a mess?"

"I don't know. Why don't you fucking clean it?"

We let things slide a lot around here. The fact that we rent only adds to our decided lack of interest in house matters; by the time we moved here to seek our fortune, a starter home with bars on the windows in a crummy neighborhood cost $550,000, at least two class levels out of our price range. We like our rental house, but will only go so far for its sake. If the toilet clogs, I can unclog it, but if the toilet breaks, we call our landlord, an amiable retired high school history teacher named Irv. He lives in Woodland Hills and, except for the month every year that he spends photographing architectural wonders in the Middle East, seems to have a lot of free time.

We try to summon Irv as little as possible. Jobs that should take twenty minutes often take two hours. He likes to sit on the stairs to my office and talk to me, like a progressive, worldly Mr. Roper. I would say that I fill some sort of filial role for him, but he has a son about my age whom he talks to all the time. Since Irv also e-mails me at least three jokes a day, I've had a good dose of him by the time he arrives. In addition, he doesn't like to pay professionals, so he does the repairs himself. Since he's not that great at repairs, sometimes he brings over a strange man in overalls, who also isn't that great at repairs. They've tried to fix our leaky garbage disposal at least a half dozen times. For a while, there was some smelly ooze coming out from underneath our toilet. They fixed that, but now the toilet sits at an angle so that if the bathroom door opens while I'm on the can, it hits me in the knees. Like sand through an hourglass, these are the days of our lives.

Our house-resentment equation is constantly being recalculated. Regina wishes I'd cook sometimes. I wish she'd clean out the garbage can in her office more than once a month and stop leaving her dirty panties on the magazine rack in the bathroom. As I write this, there's a pile of clean laundry sitting on one of the living room chairs. Every day, the pile gets bigger, because every day, Regina adds clothes.

She washes, I fold. We made this demarcation long ago, after I ruined one of her bras. But lately, Regina has been making little side comments to our son, like, "Look, Elijah, there's a big pile of laundry on the chair that Dad is supposed to fold but hasn't yet." The problem, I want to tell Regina, is that I like to fold clothes while watching a ball game, and we're in the middle of the All-Star Break. Also, I want to add, that pile sat on our bedroom floor for at least ten days before you got around to washing it, so don't go getting all high-and-mighty with me.

I feel that I do my share around the house. Often, I wonder if Regina feels the same way about me. For the purposes of researching this highly professional essay, I asked her.

"Well," she said, "you nag a lot."

"I do more than nag," I said.

"You tidy, but you don't see dirt. And you like things to be tidy according to what your brain thinks is tidy. As long as something is shoved in a closet or a drawer, and the drawer or closet closes, it's nice and tidy."

"What's wrong with that?"

"Everything. To this day, you still don't know where stuff goes when you take it out of the dishwasher, even though you've been emptying the dishwasher for nearly two years. Or for two weeks you'll get it right and then you'll start misplacing it again. It boggles my mind."

"Don't I do anything right?"

"You're very good at picking up cups that people are drinking from and putting them in the kitchen sink before they're done drinking."

"That's a negative disguised as a positive."

"You would never think of watering plants or mopping the floor. I pay all the bills, do all the grocery shopping, most of the cooking. You're not handy around the house except for a few specific things. . . . "

"Let me defend myself here. If the vacuum makes a rare appearance, it's because I bring it out. I clean the bathroom, do the dishes when I feel like it, and take care of garbage."

"Acknowledged. Also, did I mention that you nag all the time?"

"Back atcha, baby."

Child care is the only place we meet with complete equanimity. These duties, the feeding and the bathing and the driving and the discipline and the endless hours of Uno, we share fifty-fifty, with little conflict. We may not want to spend our extra home time sucking up dust bunnies, but we do want to spend it with our kid.

Sometimes, though, we go out without the kid. We don't do a regular "date night," because that kind of seems like a cliché, and we rarely feel like paying a fifty-dollar-plus babysitting charge to grab a margarita and see *The Incredible Hulk*. If we do get a sitter, it's because we get invited to a party. That happens about twice a year.

Mostly, we give each other turns. We're home together all day, so we have no trouble being apart at night. Regina meets girlfriends for drinks. I go to crappy punk-rock shows or Dodger games, or get stoned and go to a bar where I drink club soda, because that's a more economical way to party. This agreement allows us to maintain a modified version of the heedlessly selfish social lives of the child-free. We can behave on the spur of the moment with only two or three days' advance notice.

Case in point: a few days ago our friend Ryan e-mailed. He's one of the two thousand people in Los Angeles who earn a little money writing online movie reviews, and he had an extra ticket to an IMAX screening of a blockbuster superhero flick. Elijah has two parents who think superhero movies are *amazing,* so Ryan left the invitation open to both of us. It was pretty much the movie of the summer, but desperate to build up capital since our discussion about my apparent slackitude around the house, I handed this one to Regina.

"Are you sure?" she asked.

"Yes," I said.

"Oh, *awesome,*" she said, and I knew I'd done well.

"You're going to have to feed the boy," she said.

"Not a problem," I said. "I can cook."

A few hours later I was puttering around the kitchen, getting out my ingredients and trying to keep everything organized so I could cook with the efficiency of a TV chef. Elijah sat in the adjoining living room, watching *Word Girl* on PBS and eating a bowl of frozen green beans.

Regina had chosen the evening's fare. Of late, she's been obsessed with Dr. Gillian, the host of a BBC show called *You Are What You Eat,* to the point that she ordered a Dr. Gillian cookbook and has been preparing our meals based on Dr. Gillian's recommendations. Tonight, it would be baked salmon with spinach and leeks.

I wasn't happy about cooking this meal. Baked salmon is

so very early-bird special. I don't like the way it smells, or the way the little globules of fat gather on the surface while it bakes. It reeks of grossness, like the second-to-last meal you eat before you die. I walked around, eyeing the food without enthusiasm and swatting at flies.

Elijah came into the kitchen.

"Daddy?" he asked. "Can I help you make dinner?"

Sometimes, children are a sweet, helpful, friendly delight. Other times, they're despicable monsters. I'm glad Good Elijah had decided to make an appearance this time.

"Of course!" I said.

First, we washed his hands. At camp that day, he'd colored them, on both sides, with Magic Markers, because his best friend had done the same thing. Elijah is the kind of kid who copies his friends because he wants to make them happy. As I scrubbed the backs of his hands with a rough sponge, I reminded myself to give him a lecture on codependence in about a decade. Hopefully, I'll remember, because my Franklin Covey date book doesn't go ten years into the future.

Then I had him drop several handfuls of uncooked spinach into a colander. He asked me if he could eat one leaf, so I washed it special for him, and he nodded in approval. Then I produced a vegetable-wash spray gun, which looked suspiciously like bathroom cleaner.

"Nooooo!" Elijah said. "You'll poison our food."

"It's not poison," I said, in my best grown-up voice, and I showed him how to spray. We squirted the gunk on the spinach, and then I showed him how to put the colander in the salad spinner and how to add water and spin. This he loved, and we probably washed the spinach about three times more than necessary. Then again, you can't really wash spinach too much.

Next, I showed him the trick of slapping a flat knife atop a garlic clove and peeling off the skin. Elijah thought this was a bad idea, because I would cut myself. I assured him that I wouldn't, and then he suddenly grew very bored and wandered off to make his *Star Wars* figures pretend to kill each other. I slogged my way through the recipe, realizing early on that it wasn't going to taste very good. Before I even put it in the oven, I could smell the fat globules.

While I did the prep, Elijah wandered in and out of the kitchen, asking for things. He wanted to shred some cheddar cheese into a bowl. We did that, and then he ate the cheese. He wanted me to fill up his rocket-shaped bubble blower. That we also did. He took the blower outside. At some point, he was in the bathroom screaming that he couldn't find the toilet paper. All this occurred within ten minutes or so.

Finally, the quinoa was ready. I sat him down with a big bowl of the stuff, soaked it in soy sauce, and he started gulping it down. The salmon came out of the oven, nearly raw. It went back in for five minutes, and I continued to distract the boy with quinoa, which, as we all now know, is an infinitely healthy grain eaten by the human family since the dawn of time.

Five minutes later the fish was done, but the spinach and leeks had withered away to limp, waterless brownish-green approximations of their former selves. I dished the fish and the half-spinach pieces onto Elijah's plate, trying to pretend that this was not only a healthy dinner, but a delicious one as well.

Elijah ate two bites of fish and two bites of spinach, declared it too "lemony," and dug back into his quinoa. I had half the fish, which tasted as disgusting as it looked, reminding myself that there was salami in the fridge for later. We finished our dinner and I turned the oven to warm, putting the rest in for Regina for when she came back from the movie.

From there, the evening involved walking the dogs, during which Elijah removed his shirt midwalk for no reason. There was also a horseplay session during which Elijah proclaimed that hitting someone with a pillow would incur the loss of points even though I had no idea we were playing for points, and a shower, during which the following occurred:

Elijah asked for a couple minutes of "privacy." I gave it to him. When I opened the door, he had the sprayer in his mouth and a dark blue wet washcloth on his head.

"What are you doing?" I said.

"The chlorine from all my swimming turned my hair blue," he said.

"That's nice, son," I said.

I turned around to get some soap. When I looked back, he'd moved the washcloth down his forehead and across his eyes.

"Look, Daddy, my hair is growing," he said.

The dude got tickled mercilessly for that one. Then, after pajamas and a Popsicle came a session with a Level One reading primer about a mouse trying to fix a leaky faucet. I tried to get Elijah to read, but he screamed that he didn't feel like sounding out words because his mouth was very dry. This battle could wait for another time, or, even better, another decade. After that, it was my turn to read Tintin in *The Crab with the Golden Claws*, and I had to explain to the boy, for the twentieth time, the meaning of opium smuggling. We also both continued to marvel at Tintin's ability to emerge from airplane crashes unharmed. A cup of ice water and a lullaby CD later, the boy was in bed, if not actually asleep, and we'd gotten him through another day alive.

All the while, the kitchen smelled of fish, a horrible smell, like the entire dish had turned into leaky salmon fat. Now, I removed the fish from the oven. Apparently, "warm" means "bake until unrecognizable." The fish had turned bright orange and was very dry. Sadly, it now tasted better than it had before. I seethed, not at myself, but at Regina's anticipated reaction when she came home from the movie. "I fucking slaved over a hot stove for hours," I said to myself.

Regina didn't care when she got home, enraptured as she was by the leading man's magnificent performance. She ate quinoa without complaint and gave me a plot summary. Only later, as I sat in my basement sucking on my vaporizer, did she broach the salmon.

"You know, you were supposed to make an avocado miso dressing," she said.

"I didn't know if we had the ingredients," I said.

"What?" she said. "You can't read a simple recipe?"

"I guess not," I said.

"It would have tasted better."

"No," I said. "The dish was shit, whether or not it was dressed up with avocado miso whatever, and I fucking made it and it didn't turn out well, and you can drop the topic right now before I really get angry."

"Okay," she said.

"My neck is really sore," I said. "Can you massage it in bed?"

"Sure," she said. "Really? You couldn't follow a recipe?"

"Drop it."

A half hour later, I came to bed. The wife was nearly asleep.

"I need my massage," I said.

"You missed your window," she said.

I sighed, saying something like "I always miss my window," and went to sleep a lonely househusband. In our situation, where the roles of mother and father, man and woman have completely merged, shattering all cultural constructs, Regina and I evenly share desperate feelings of domestic uselessness. It doesn't feel good at the time, but making up is easier.

The next day, unbidden, Regina came up to me and opened her arms for a hug.

"To what do I owe this pleasure?" I asked.

"I'm just so proud of you and everything you do," she said.

Sometimes, it's good to be home together all day.

12.
Love, Money, and the Unmarried Couple Judith Levine

A marriage may or may not be a union of love. It is always a union of property. No matter how you conduct your affairs—joint or separate checking accounts; rooms, even homes, of your own—the state regards you as a unit. The day you sign the license, you and your spouse are taxed as one. And if you break up, you become half of one: it divides your wealth in two. Prenuptial agreements can prevent the foregoing, but prenups are not always enforced (and they never supersede child-support laws). Anyway, lots of people find prenups distasteful. Marriage, they feel, is about love, not property.

Paul and I have been together for seventeen years. Neither of us has ever been married, and we don't intend to marry each other. There are no practical reasons to do so—no kids (unless you count our elderly diabetic cat, Julius), no employer-paid health insurance—and several tax-related reasons not to.

The reasons we've resisted marriage differ. Paul's are

fairly straightforward. Periodically, he's looked around at married couples and found them no happier or more committed than unmarried couples. My own reasons are more ideological, but the ideology has a burning strain of emotion. An old-fashioned anarchist-feminist, I despise the idea of the state legitimizing my personal or sexual liaisons. I'd like the state to get out of the sexual-licensing business altogether, actually, for couples gay, straight, bi, or none of the above. But as long as all of the above can't take advantage of the institution, I won't either.

I don't want to oversimplify marriage or romanticize living together. The former isn't a static or mindless category of the unexamined life; the latter isn't a full-time orgy of keeping love alive. But marriage, to me, offers a ready-made commitment I'd rather go without. I prefer having to make the choice to be, or not to be, with the person I am involved with, to remember, without the aid of a gold band or the vision of dueling divorce lawyers, why I am with that person.

Mainly, though, my aversion to marriage is about love and property. Marriage creates a kind of human property. Women may no longer be chattel; in spite of ongoing wage inequality, most wives are neither their husbands' emotional slaves nor their economic dependents (thanks to feminism). Still, marriage implies ownership: each spouse owns the other. I have never craved an identity or a relationship that can be named only in the possessive: "*my* husband, *my* wife."

As for material property, I'm uninterested in forming a limited-partner corporation in bride's and groom's clothing.

And just as I don't want the state blessing my union, I'd like to avoid it dividing the spoils should that union fail.

A love relationship between unmarried people who live together is not legally a partnership of property, and that's how I like it. I think of myself as one of the least romantic people on earth. But just like those romantics at the altar, I don't want to mix love and money.

And yet, money is rarely far from any consequential personal pairing—not just between boss and worker or landlord and tenant, but between parent and child, friends or lovers. Relationships are enacted through talk and touch; they are deepened by shared experiences. But, like civilizations since the beginning of time, they are also sustained through the exchange of goods and services, credit and cash, often held out as gifts or punishment. When a parent wants to show her disapproval, she may deny a child a toy or treat. When a lover wants to show affection, he may take his partner to her favorite restaurant. In the first case a feeling is demonstrated by not spending money, in the latter by spending it.

People in relationships not only give and receive (or withhold) items bought with money, they also buy and use items together. Married or not, the longer two people share a life, the more central to that life property becomes. Stuff, like a couple, merges.

Paul and I met in 1991. Like any new couple, we each paid our way. It was simple. We each had a car and a home with a mortgage, taxes, and maintenance to support. When we bought groceries to cook together, when we ate out or went to the movies, we split the cost down the middle. Since we earned about the same amount—he as a nonprofit political and energy consultant, I as a writer and editor—what was simple was also fair. And since neither of us earns a lot and our incomes fluctuate from year to year, our consumption styles were also compatible. We both have learned to keep the overhead low, the financial view long, and the gratification delayed.

These facts were additionally important for us, even at the start. We were both thirty-nine, living in two states—I in an apartment in Brooklyn, New York, he in a house in northeastern Vermont—so whenever we were together, we were living together. Those periods together got longer fast. The first year I spent the whole summer in Vermont; soon I was spending a couple of months in the winter there, too, and Paul was coming to New York often. In both places we work at home, so when we are together, we are rarely apart.

With so much proximity, our stuff began to merge. The little things were the first to do so. For instance, I had six green-and-yellow 1950s highball glasses. One by one they broke, until there were two. One afternoon, browsing a crockery store, we came upon some jaunty tall polka-dot glasses on sale. We picked up four, one of us paid with plastic and wrote the sum in our cookie-jar tally. When we settled up, the cost of the glasses was added in along with bread and rice and movie tickets. Now, many years later, we have six tall glasses. Do the green-and-yellow ones still belong to me? Or were they grandfathered in under unspoken joint-property bylaws?

Our books, CDs, dishes, linens, tools, plants, and furniture mingled too. Some of the books are obviously his (anything about electricity or Vermont politics); some are clearly mine (anything about feminism). But what about the bird guides, the Thai and Jewish cookbooks? To whom did the Beatles' *White Album* CD belong? Who paid for the tablecloth in Lisbon? Who can remember?

Business expenses started bundling: pens and envelopes, a cell phone contract, a DSL line. Each purchase requires calculation. Is it practical (is this expense best kept separate, for accounting purposes)? Is it fair (will s/he use the cell phone much more than I do)? Each asks for a measure of generosity (so what if he uses the cell phone more than I do? I use more envelopes). Each needs to trust that the other will not overspend his or her share.

But a hundred-pack of envelopes is not going to break the budget for either of us, even if the other person ends up using ninety-nine envelopes. It was not until my car died, then, that generosity and trust truly were tested. My eleven-year-old Volkswagen Golf, with 166,000 miles on it, broke irreparably. As it happens, I was broke too. I considered borrowing money for a new car but was already almost eight thousand dollars in debt. Paul had money in the bank. He offered to buy the car. We found a four-year-old Honda Civic in good shape, for sixty-five hundred dollars. I put in a thousand dollars. He picked up the rest.

This decision wasn't automatic. Paul had to think about making the offer, and I had to think about accepting it. Would there be a quid pro quo? Would I feel perpetually guilty or he resentful if I never got around to returning the favor? We couldn't be sure. Still, talking about the car gave us an opportunity to talk about money, which we had rarely done. Paul knew I worried about money, but until that moment I don't think he was aware of how alone I felt, or how often I panicked. We were in this together, he reassured me; he would not let me go under. Now here was concrete proof.

The car meant more to me than it might have if we were married, because it was a gift, not an obligation. But it did not signal that everything would change. Paul wouldn't let me go under, but neither was he indicating that I could blithely dive in over my head and expect him to save me from drowning every time. I felt relieved but not rescued, grateful but not complacent.

A year later, I bought an apartment, and my lawyer suggested I write a will. Just doing so, he said, was a chance to think about what and whom I cared about, in the form of where I wanted my property to end up. I gave a few pieces of art and furniture to friends and set aside some cash for my niece and nephew, as well as several political causes I feel passionate about. The rest of my money and the apartment—my only real and valuable property—I left to Paul. Eventually, Paul wrote a will too, leaving his house, land, and cash to me.

We had not vowed to stay together until death us do part (in fact, we had only been together seven years when I bought my apartment). Yet our wills were testament to that expectation. Paradoxically, it was an extended experiment in *not* consuming that revealed a lot about Paul's and my relationship to money and to each other through money. In

2004, we purchased nothing but necessities (basic groceries, insulin for Julius the cat, Internet access, toilet paper) and eschewed the rest (new clothes, books, CDs, restaurant meals, theater tickets, travel). I kept track, meditated on the meanings, both personal and political, of the consumer culture, and wrote about it. I wondered, could a person get off the wheel of getting and spending, even if she wanted to? Could she have not just a job, but a social, cultural, or family life, even an identity without buying? If the answer was no, where could solutions be found to the huge global economic and social problems wrought by overconsumption?

One thing I figured out right away was that I wanted no part of an anticonsumerist movement that encouraged, even unwittingly, a feeling of righteous superiority in its adherents or mobilized conversion to its tenets through guilt. How could we cut back in our household without moral competition or shame?

I had the feeling Paul would be better at abstention than I. He is temperamentally a nonshopper. A rural boy from a penurious family, he'd rather spend a day a month retwisting and soldering the coils of an ancient toaster than purchase a new one with micromanaged darkness scales and bagel-size slots. Paul can go a year without a movie. He has been known to darn his socks.

As for me, while I think of myself as a desultory and uncommitted consumer at best, I do love my stuff. I don't own a dishwasher, riding mower, or microwave oven, and I have just one thirteen-inch television; in 2004 I didn't have a cell phone. Yet I think nothing of forking over ten bucks to view any obscure French avant-garde feminist film that passes through New York or fifteen dollars for an hour and a quarter of yoga instruction, half of which time I do little more than breathe. I buy the no-name tampons, yet I unswervingly maintain that the two hundred milligrams of pure ibuprofen in an Advil capsule cures my headache faster than a two-hundred-milligram capsule of pure ibuprofen in the bottle labeled "Ibuprofen," which costs half as much. In my pantry, I have three kinds of salt.

I started out the year with a sense of inferiority. Paul was already better at earning and managing money than I. I already worried more about earning and spending than he did. I was worried that now I'd be worse at not spending too.

In spite of his selective consumer fetishes, including a devotion to fine spirits that led to the startling (and, to me, comforting) admission that he was willing to spend sixty dollars on a bottle of good Scotch, Paul did sail pretty effortlessly through the year. Besides wine and beer (which he started brewing at home), he missed not much more than Q-tips. I missed a few things—movies and ice cream, for instance—but to my surprise, I missed participation in the whole consumer culture. My identity was staked on being in the know—seeing the new movies, reading the new books. My social life was conducted, more than I'd realized, in cafés and bars. And though I had never in my life gone shopping for entertainment, I found I missed the act of buying things. Even the small amount of shopping that I do provides a goal for a walk in the neighborhood; it supplies a little thrill in hunting down the perfect thing, a pleasant social connection as money and chat are exchanged with the merchant, and a happy satisfaction in bringing the thing home, admiring it, and putting it away.

So, eight months into the year, I lapsed. In town on a hot afternoon with a half hour on my hands, I strolled into a clothing store. What seduced me was not just an elegant yet comfortable pair of green pants, but a skilled and sexy sales-woman. We flirted, she, I, and the beckoning item of clothing. Then I abandoned hope of restraint and bought the pants.

Meeting up with Paul afterward, I confessed. "It was an impulse buy," I said. (This was a lie; I committed the crime with malice aforethought.)

He did not scold, he did not gloat. Rather, he paused and thought. "You know, I've been in therapy ten years trying to be more impulsive," he said. Again, I'd had him wrong. He had no interest in judging me. Indeed, he judged himself: for him, constant holding back was a problem, not a source of pride.

We emerged from the year feeling more secure about the future, realizing how happily we could live on very little. I did not worry about money all year. Neither of us was shocked or repelled by the other's needs or desires. And though the project was largely about the use (or not) of money, we did not once fight about or even discuss it.

On January 1, 2005, I rented six movies and binge-watched them (Paul fell asleep during half of them). He rushed out for a box of Q-tips. When we returned to the city from Vermont, we went directly to Zaytoon's, our favorite neighborhood restaurant, where we shared a falafel plate with baba ghanoush, salad, and hot, freshly made pita. Adding to the satisfaction, we washed it down with Paul's home-brewed amber ale—and ran into a couple of friends we hadn't seen in months. The tab came to seven dollars plus tax and tip. Delectable, healthy food at great value, beautiful waitresses, a welcome-back atmosphere even for first-time patrons: Zaytoon's offers sensual pleasures and a sense of community and lets us support the local economy, to boot. Was the meal a necessity or a luxury? Neither. It came to our table, redolent and tempting, at the meeting place of the two. It was also where Paul's and my desires and values meet.

The year did not resolve every issue of love and money. Indeed, just before we embarked on scaling down, we had launched a project of scaling up—an addition and major renovation to our Vermont house. Nonconsumption had temporarily wiped money off the agenda. The project put it back on, big-time.

The renovation would finally transform a one-man house to a home and workplace for two or more. No longer would Paul's office dominate the corner of our bedroom, its boxes and papers threatening to devour the entire space. No longer would I work at a desk in the downstairs hallway, impeding passage between kitchen and living room and subjecting my concentration to disturbances by any visitor or conversation in the rest of the house. Our guests would have a room of their own, and no more nights on a lumpy foldout couch. And the cellar would cease to flood.

But eating Sheetrock dust for months or (in our case) years, watching the bills mount, arguing over whether the cabinet doors should be made of pine or plywood, or a million other details—in the best of circumstances, home improvement is a notorious home wrecker. Marriages founder when homes are under renovation, as partners recognize that their desires and needs (or their tolerance for mess and inconvenience) don't mesh. The same is true for unmarriages like Paul's and mine. What's more, for people who live together but do not share a bank account, big expensive projects also bring up questions that casual financial arrangements can't address.

The house was Paul's—his investment, his equity; its small mortgage was nearly paid off. So he priced the hired-out parts of the job and estimated material costs, time, and other labor, most of which he planned to do himself. He figured it would take one year, two at most. Then he calculated the size of a refinanced mortgage.

But the demands of Paul's paying job got in the way of the unpaid labor of the renovation. As the second summer ended with less than half the work finished, I started feeling like a prisoner in a construction site surrounded by a moat of mud. I felt misled. I took to having temper tantrums, alternately declaring my regrets that we'd ever started and nagging Paul to get someone in to finish it. But it was Paul's money. Without consulting me, he had decided how much to spend on hired labor.

I offered to pay a carpenter. Paul resisted. Without his oversight, he felt, the job would be shoddy. I was at his mercy. But he was also at mine, he pointed out, because just as the craftsmanship had to meet his Olympian standards, the aesthetics had to live up to mine; that meant extensive consideration, reconsideration, and debate.

By the third year, I was frantic. "We'll have a gorgeous house, and then we'll break up," I predicted during one teary fight. He agreed that the tension was getting to be too much. He hired Joe the carpenter, and I contributed to his pay. Often, Paul and Joe worked together; sometimes Joe worked alone. Some of the work was not perfect, but most of it was fine and some of it excellent. By the end of the fourth summer, everything but the back porch and the bathrooms was finished.

That fourth year, too, the "feminine" part of the job—my part—began. I shopped for paint and fabric and picture frames; I put the charges on my credit card. The loan was exhausted anyway, and Paul was drawing on savings. So we split more of the costs. For years, as I spent more and more time in Vermont, I had been putting my stamp on the house and land. When I wanted a perennial garden, Paul and a friend dug a long bed around a rock ledge. From then on, the flower garden was mine to tend, and to finance. I drove Paul's old Chevy pickup to auctions and lugged home a funky table here, a jelly cabinet or antique vase there, on my dime. Now we jointly bought a bed, a sofa, and a rug, at a total of more than five thousand dollars.

After much arguing and compromising, we both adore the house. And, though it is still in Paul's name, it is *our* home. Emotionally and financially we are in deep—together.

A good friend of mine—I'll call him Mike—just broke up with his girlfriend, "Jenny." At the start of their relationship, Mike had moved into Jenny's New York co-op, which she'd bought ten years earlier. They lived together for ten years, during which time he paid half the mortgage and did work on the place, sharing the cost of materials and new appliances. The apartment's value increased enormously, in part because of the improvements Mike made, in part because of the astronomical rises in New York real estate. Although it was never formalized legally, Mike and Jenny planned to retire together by selling the apartment and moving to a cheaper place out of the city.

But then things soured between Mike and Jenny. She felt their problems could be repaired; he did not and ended up leaving her.

Mike believes it's only fair that Jenny repay him for his contribution to the apartment, in which she has gained equity. He has always known her to be an honest and upright person, and there was talk of settling up when they first considered splitting. But Jenny has made no move to pay Mike. Maybe she is getting back at him, with the only weapon she has. Maybe she feels that her financial injustice equals his emotional injustice.

These days, divorce courts rarely calculate the dollar value of pain. In divorce, the judge splits the joint wealth down the middle. If there are children, the judge looks at the income, earning potential, and expenses of each parent, then calibrates child support.

What if the stresses and disappointments of the coupled life threatened to overwhelm Paul's and my love? What would hold us together? We have no kids. While we'd forfeit some of the comfort we now enjoy, both of us would be able to support ourselves, as we did before we met. We have seventeen years' history together, and that is nothing to sneeze at—but we also, I hope, have decades ahead of us.

A set of glasses, a sofa, a rug, even a house cannot prevent the alienation of two people from each other. Still, I'd be lying were I to claim that property has nothing to do with why, and how, we stay together. The house is more than a building. It is a monument to our mutual struggles and pleasures, our fears and our security. In the hard-fought shape and size of its rooms and hallways, the lovingly chosen colors of its walls, the books and photos on its shelves, our names are engraved on the house, side by side, and forever will be.

We are still working it out, this tricky interaction of love and money. Paul has suggested a joint checking account, which he sees as a way to further our unity. I see it as a means of surveillance and a potential source of bickering. How much independence is healthy? What abets commitment, what undermines it?

Having finished my fourth book, I am reassessing my career. I'd like to take more time to learn new media, collaborate on creative projects, read and think—activities that are not likely to earn money. Would Paul support me, even for a few months? Should I do all the housework as compensation? Would he expect that from me—or secretly hope that I'll return the favor in the future? What if I can never afford to?

When Paul bought me the car, I felt saved but not entirely safe, like family but not quite. Maybe that's a good thing—better than assuming a future that is by no means guaranteed. After all, parents do not always bail out their children, adult children do not always take care of their aged parents. Divorced women often end up poor. How much security is reasonable to expect?

The questions are the same as they were in the first years of our life together. What is practical? What is fair? And they are different. Should Paul and I aim for perfect financial equality? Or does that quest betray—or even encourage—the suspicion that one is putting in more than her share and the other taking advantage?

It is still not easy to answer these questions or even, after fifteen years, to talk about them, because for Paul and me, as for most of us, money has a childhood history; it represents identity, status, independence, security, and—when exchanged or shared between intimates—love.

We will probably never finish working it out. In the meantime, for better or worse, for richer or poorer, we are pulling tighter the knot we never legally tied.

13.
Unassisted Sasha Hom

I am sitting in a café in Davis, California. One of my babies sleeps beside me; the other is kicking soccer balls on a field on the other side of town. My husband is across the Pacific Ocean, following our dream of learning another land. We are a family with a blueprint for wandering inscribed on the soles of our feet. Languages are embedded there, waiting to be spoken. Sometimes the blueprint has created safe passage. Other times, we have been tossed about, scraped raw by the sand.

Five years ago, when I was twenty-nine years old, jobless, pregnant, and sprawled across pillows on the floor of my midwife's houseboat, I felt it important to tell my midwife about my dreams of flight, of soaring. I always landed, I told her. Sometimes with a thud, my limbs jerking as I awoke, or gracefully on two feet. Then I'd rise up, dragging my wings, and walk slowly into wakefulness.

My soon-to-be husband and I looked around the room at six other pregnant couples sitting on a circle of cushions, taking turns asking questions and voicing fears like rolling dice onto the middle of the floor. We were six, five, and nine and a half months pregnant and counting. One woman on the verge of labor moaned softly. Someone's husband dreamed of the death of the family cat. A couple argued over the wife's sugar consumption, struggling to control the uncontrollable.

Our midwife didn't run her practice conventionally. Instead of meeting her clients individually once or twice a month, she met all of us every Sunday evening in her houseboat. When she asked how we had arrived at our decision to have a home birth, neither of us knew what to say. How to explain that, like a dowser searching for deep waters, we are guided by intuition, luck, science, and words spoken between us in our sleep? That we paid attention to the story beneath the surface and allowed it to shape our lives? That our practice of balancing attention and surrender, like sitting on a surfboard watching the swell, enabled us to choose how to give birth to our first child?

We didn't plan our pregnancy, just as Dylan says he never planned on proposing to me, he just couldn't stop the words. We were living in a converted garage in Forestville that flooded when it drizzled, which amid the redwoods was often. We sat staring at an orange mushroom that had sprung up in the corner of the rug. We toyed with the idea of having children within the year. He spoke of trepidation about supporting a family. But our bodies already knew what they wanted, and as we planned and feared, a small thing flip-flopped inside of me, with a name like the sound of waves pulling stones back into the sea.

Soon, we wouldn't have a place to live. We put an ad on Craigslist: *Pregnant couple with aging pit bull searching for a room in your house to give birth in. Usually quiet and clean. Unemployed with references.* No one replied. I joked that if the hospital were a nicer place than we ended up living, I would prefer to give birth in a hospital.

We went to the doctor when we found out. We told him we didn't want an ultrasound or tests or exams. We just wanted to talk and ask questions. The nurse told me to take off everything but my socks and wait in a cold curtained room. Eventually, she came back, pulling a computer on a cart, and as she opened the door, I saw another woman in the room across the hall wearing an identical gown, with her socks on, sitting on the examining table alone in a hollow room.

Later, we decided to forgo all medical interventions including ultrasounds, blood tests, and vaccinations. We saw how making fear-based decisions only opened us to more fear. Who were we to say what the experience of birth should be, or that it is even preferable for every baby to be born healthy? Who were we to say that life should look a certain way to preclude parental suffering, and that our baby should be the one passed over by death at the moment when death and life cling together?

I don't believe in debating whether life is defined by fate or free will. What I know is that life often feels like a circle, though at the midwife's, sitting in the circle of pregnancy, it sometimes felt more linear, a different kind of conveyor belt that moved us along and dropped us into the unknown in pairs. One week we'd arrive on her houseboat and two pairs of shoes would be missing by the door. Then, with no questions asked, we'd take our seat among a group of six couples instead of the seven that had been there the week before. Next time, there would be five, then four, until someone new arrived and took their own place in the circle.

The first two hours of our Sunday evenings were spent "checking in" or listening to a birth story. Afterward, we opened our backpacks and shared our snacks, like breaking bread on a scuffed softwood floor, to consecrate what each person was experiencing, from housing issues to gestational diabetes, with challah or trail mix. By then the sun was setting.

Outside, the night herons perched on the moorings, peering into the water and waiting for the right moment to dive. Inside, we took turns climbing onto a nest of pillows, raising our shirts just enough for the midwife to put her ear to our bellies and hear the rhythm of our growing children. She listened to the heartbeat with her naked ear, and translated for us its language. "*Que preciosa*," she told Dylan and me, "sleeping with a hand by the face."

The first time we joined our midwife's circle, we hadn't yet decided to work with her. In fact, we had already agreed to work with another pair of midwives who worked with their clients one on one: meetings once a month until the second trimester, twice a month until the third, assistance with nutrition and supplements when needed. But, by joining the circle, we shared what can be too much for one person to hold. And we spoke aloud our commitment to community, each other, and letting go of control.

That first day, a beautiful woman on the verge of labor wept openly. Her baby had turned breech, her husband was traveling, and her family had pressured her to have a Cesarean. The following week we heard that she birthed her breech baby girl—vaginally, naturally, at home—and the baby died. One couple, due around the same time as us, was deeply affected by the news, and decided to have their birth at the hospital. On a Sunday afternoon months later we learned that a knot in the umbilical cord stopped the flow of oxygen to their baby's brain, and he passed away peacefully under the care of both a doctor and a midwife.

Dylan and I found a one-room studio cottage to rent on the border of Oakland and Berkeley. It was in a neighborhood I could see myself walking during labor, and the floors of the cottage were tiled for easy cleanup. We began to prepare by loading batches of chicken stock into the freezer, easy-to-eat foods into the cupboard, and making a list of phone numbers of people who could take the dog. But I started to have dreams that birth would sneak up on me when no one was looking. These dreams stuck to me during my waking hours, like maternity dresses in the August heat.

I first noticed warm liquid running down my leg on a Wednesday night. We put the rubber sheet on the foam mattress just in case, but remembered the woman who didn't go into labor until three days after her water broke. Dylan immediately went to sleep because he knew that if I went into labor, he'd have a lot of work to do.

I couldn't sleep. At first, I lay in bed worrying about the

neighbors, and listening to the rats scuttling across our roof and between the walls. I worried that a crowd of relatives would form outside the door waiting to flood our studio apartment. I worried that the car wouldn't start if I had to be transported to the hospital, or that the dog would be freaked out by the birth.

The pain of early labor was familiar, like coming off seven hits of acid acutely aware of your partner next to you snoring. I tried to remember what we had learned in our childbirth class, but even then, I could never keep the different stages of labor straight, how long contractions were supposed to be, or what was supposed to happen when.

I woke Dylan after I had expelled what seemed like a small Porta-Potty's worth of fluids from my body and could no longer keep myself warm. He brought out what we thought was a heater left by the previous tenants only to find out it was a humidifier. He turned on the stove and made himself breakfast as I felt the fear cramping my muscles and doubted my ability to withstand the pain.

Our midwife came at 9:30 a.m. Dylan helped her open the collapsible birth tub and move a few things around so it could fit at the foot of the bed next to the kitchen sink. We didn't have a way to fill it, so Dylan went out and borrowed the neighbor's garden hose, duct-taped it to the sink, and began the two-hour process of slowly filling the one-hundred-fifty-gallon tub. I was only three centimeters dilated. "You still have a ways to go," our midwife said. "These are your last moments to be together as just a couple."

She gave us a list of signs that would indicate I'd progressed and should give her a call. I didn't want her to leave. I was afraid. I didn't know what to do with my contractions and she told me how to let them take my body off the ground, then run with my breath and out my toes like water draining.

I call it a possession akin to pain, but not quite pain. I didn't feel pain; I was pain, a sensation that kept me hungry for eyes. My husband's eyes were like birds; they were the only things offering air. I wasn't flying and I wasn't falling. I was expanding past the walls—a vast space filled with stars and the sound of water constantly running. This expansion was simultaneously constricting, and my eyes would roll into the back of my head from the splitting while I gasped for air and roared like a bull. Dylan said I looked as if I were seeing spirits. Then my eyes would close and I'd fall into a deep sleep.

These contractions came in sets like waves no longer than thirty seconds. A couple of short ones, then a lull that I'd sleep through while Dylan ran around trying to expedite the process of filling the birth tub. We were working so hard. It took so much effort for me not to explode, to find what I needed in his face, to allow my body to do what it needed to do, that there was no room for fear. In this stage of active labor, the concept of "pain" couldn't enter my consciousness because there was no room for consciousness. It was all being.

We can't really say when it began because we were just there, and everything was just there, as it always is. So when something began to poke out of me, then recede, and then bulge, with the rhythm of my expanding body, we didn't take notice. I thought I was pooping on the bed, and hoping the tub would fill so I could get in the water and wash it all away. Then, finally the tub did fill and I went to use the bathroom before getting in. I began to squat over the toilet when I was overcome by another contraction and I grabbed Dylan's shoulders for support. All of a sudden there was this squishy thing sticking out of me and I could feel it with my hand and see it in the mirror. I thought it was my liver or my spleen or part of my large intestine.

Dylan said to get into the birth tub and I suggested he give the midwife's assistant a call. As he got on the phone, I stepped into the tub. It was 11:30 in the morning, two hours after the midwife had visited. He was on the phone with her assistant and though I don't remember letting out this primal guttural roar, the assistant remembered the sound days later and the thought, "That sounds like a woman in active labor," that came with it.

On my knees in the water, I watched a gray object shoot out of me. It soared through the air with its arms spread out like a superhero and its back toward the starless sky. My very first thought was, "flying squirrel." Like Rocky in *Rocky and Bullwinkle* she soared, then twisted underwater to face me. Without thinking, I scooped her up, water spilling out around her in drops, and I put her purple body on my chest. My husband hung up on the assistant and climbed into the tub just as our daughter let out a cry like a call to arms.

The midwife's assistant later told us that she ran with the phone in her hand to the midwife, yelling, "The baby's been born. The baby's been born." And they got into her car and sped through every red light, rolled through every stop sign, while calmly leaving messages on our answering machine instructing us to keep the baby warm, check the cord, and clear her passageways of mucus.

We held each other in the tub, rose with her still attached to me, and climbed onto the bed, covering ourselves with blankets. The midwife arrived ten minutes later. Seven months pregnant herself, she ran down the driveway, leapt over our front neighbor's giant mastiff, and entered our home incredulously, laughing and asking us why we hadn't called her directly.

"The thought never crossed our minds."

Early in our relationship, Dylan and I lived illegally in a historic renovated bunker, among foghorns, splintered redwood beams, five-gallon buckets of water, dirty dishes hidden beneath the table, and happy mice. On yet another windy night without power, we sat next to each other on the beach in the dark, contemplating the ocean and possibility.

"What would you be if you could be something other than what you are?" I asked.

"What do you mean?" he said. That was the way it was with us at first. Like a lizard and a dog conversing in Spanish, or a Berkeley dog walker and a Rhode Island composer communicating with English. We never understood the meaning of each other's words.

"If you could live your life over, and have done exactly

what you've done, but one other thing in addition, what would that be? Like, I wish I could sing."

"Everybody can sing."

"No. No. They can't."

"Okay. I wish I had taken up surfing."

"Yeah, me too," I said.

Just then, out of the darkness, over the black sea, a humongous cruise ship slipped around the cliffs, lit up like a huge Christmas tree on its way out to the Pacific. It was breathtaking, appalling, and surreal. And then, just as quickly, it disappeared.

There was a shiver as everything returned to darkness. I looked at Dylan. Even in the dark I could see him clearly.

Then, as if by magic, the ship slowly reappeared, emerging from behind a huge rock. We began to laugh and in the opening of that laugh an arrangement was made, past decisions were abandoned, and something new began.

Perhaps that is where our journey as a nomadic family started, at that first opening we glimpsed simultaneously in the dark. Or perhaps it began on the day we drove to Bolinas, our surfboard straps rattling in the wind, the lagoon on our left, cliffs to our right, our sleeping baby in the back-seat. We felt defeated. We had come to the conclusion that a depressive-obsessive writer who believes that movement cures all and a composer/artist largely influenced by the natural world shouldn't be living like this—separated by a forty-hour-a-week job, the challenges of new mother-hood, and far too much traffic on our narrow street in Rich-mond.

With one hand on the steering wheel, the other out the window holding the straps of the surfboard to minimize the vibration, Dylan told me about his college days, and how he once imagined himself living in an RV. "Even though now I'm married with a small child, I think of it," he said. "I guess I've always been kind of slow." We looked at each other. We had heard about a 1976 veggie oil Winnebago for sale, with solar panels and its original fridge. And from the deafening sound of the straps vibrating in the wind, another road presented itself.

Within weeks we were huddled in our van, sleeping in "bunk" hammocks, one hung above the other. We began traveling between oceans with one aged pit bull, a small child and another on the way, hoarding vegetable oil for fuel. That's the way it's been with us: a constant fine-tuning of our ears, and when it's just the right pitch, the right vibration of the water, we paddle, searching out the openings in the wave.

We landed on an island in Maine, collecting recyclables, working for food, chopping vegetables, and fearing the end of our wanderings. How to continue living like nomads, on islands, in vans, writing stories and making music, because we believe family is our art, and our art is our work, and our work is a reflection of our spiritual values?

The solution we have come up with—a Ph.D. program in performance studies at UCD—is really no solution at all, but it has enabled us to have another child without another job. Our now three-year-old daughter is playing with a plastic ball on a toxic lawn, avoiding hot gusts of air from leaf blowers.

The air is thick with smog. Davis, California, is not our ideal stopping place, but it is where our second child was born, amongst these unholy winds, where we still see openings and how an ocean can disappear.

Our daughter Sora's birth was similar to Naima's— unassisted, beneath the water, at home. Except this time, I knew what to do with the pain. This time, it was an invitation rather than a possession. By the light of a single candle while my husband wept at the sight and every part of my body undulated, I felt God. I understood that to go with God, one must die many times. God is in the contractions, and I welcomed the pain of opening. I explained this to Dylan as I danced. The words were a bridge between my body and his. The pain was God and my mind was movement. I moved until God was the sun behind the clouds, and I felt the baby's presence.

"The baby is coming," I told him. But with those words, I became afraid. "How do I know it's okay to push? What if I hurt myself?"

"It's okay," he said. "Your body knows what to do."

I pushed the head to crowning, then peeled off my socks and climbed into the birth tub. I had to push some more, and that scared me too, so different than with Naima. I changed my position so that my back was to Dylan, and the baby swam out in his direction. Dylan passed her back to me and I scooped up her limp body, placid with faith in her mother, lids closed, without an independent life of her own. I was staring down at darkness. I bounced, coaxing life, rubbing the chest of death. We were not used to seeing a being so relaxed, and in that moment, where time does a funny thing, the cry of her voice was a miracle.

The next morning, Naima woke up to find us collapsed in a heap on the floor. "Oh, my sister's here," she said sleepily, as if finding a new life in her living room were the most natural thing in the world.

14.

Sharing Madison **Dawn Friedman**

The first time I met my daughter, Madison, she wasn't mine yet and I wasn't sure she would ever be. I stared into her solemn face and looked shyly at her mother, Jessica.

"Can I pick her up?" I asked.

"Of course," she said proudly.

There was nothing about Madison that was familiar—not her round face, her tuft of hair, the heft of her body. When I gazed at her, I felt enormous tenderness and the quiet stirring of potential love, but I didn't know her. And I was afraid to look too closely because I knew that, just as I had felt the shift and click of my son's life falling into place after his birth seven years before, so Jessica was coming to know Madison. All those months, she had thought she was carrying just any baby when all along it was Madison. Someone special and unique. She was saying to her daughter what I had said to my son: "Oh, it was you!"

Adoption social workers say that every woman needs to say hello to her baby before she can know if she can say good-bye. But I wanted to say hello to Madison too. I wanted to let myself fall in love with her. I wanted to unwrap her and examine each little limb, bury my face in her neck, let my fingers trail across her features. But she wasn't mine. I grieved her even as I knew she wasn't mine to grieve.

Three days after Madison's birth I watched my husband buckle her into the car seat, and then I climbed into the backseat beside her. I thought about Jessica, who we'd left sobbing in the maternity ward. I knew her arms were aching for her daughter, the daughter who was now ours.

"She's beautiful," I said to my husband. He glanced into the rearview mirror. "I know," he said. We sped through the gray morning, heading home.

"I feel like a kidnapper," I told him.

"I know," he said.

My husband and I came to open adoption filled with hopeful naiveté. We tried for several years (with several miscarriages) to have a second child, but when our fertility doctor said we might need more extensive treatment, we decided to walk away. A few months later, we began to explore adoption. Foster-to-adopt, we decided, would be too emotionally risky for ourselves and, more important, for our then six-year-old son. International adoption was too expensive. But when we found domestic infant adoption through a local nonprofit agency, we realized that we had found our way to be parents again. The agency was local and worked with expectant parents and hopeful families in-state, which meant that we wouldn't need to deal with a different state's adoption laws. Then when we talked to parents who had used the agency, we learned that they were good at hand-holding—something we were sure we'd need.

We knew that our adoption would be at least semi-open. We would be sharing our vital statistics—first names, ages, religion, as well as carefully chosen pictures—with birth mothers, as per the agency's requirements. But we wanted more. We wanted a fully open adoption with an ongoing relationship and continuing contact. We wanted holiday visits, regular phone calls, and even—dare we hope—contact with the extended birth family. We felt our baby-to-be would benefit from knowing his or her origins; we considered it a birthright. We also strongly believed birth parents were due some kind of relationship with their children and with their children's adoptive parents—if they wanted one.

We weathered the fear-mongering tales of well-intentioned friends and acquaintances, people who had watched nightly news stories of toddlers snatched by their birth parents from adoptive families who had cared for them since birth. We listened as they wondered aloud what kind of woman would have the strength to walk away from her baby and then come back for occasional visits. "What if she kidnaps the baby?" they'd say. "What if she treats you like babysitters?"

But in talking to our agency's social worker and reading more about open adoption, I learned that parents who place their children are committed to their children's well-being—that's why they make adoption plans. From what she told us, the birth parents who worked with the agency understood these boundaries and respected them. I trusted this would be true for our adoption too.

Other adoptive parents we knew chose to go abroad in

part because they were alarmed by the trend toward increasing openness in domestic infant adoptions. "Won't you feel jealous?" they'd ask. "Won't it confuse the child? What if your child likes her more than she likes you?"

Having already weathered the "I hate you" and "I'd rather live with Grandma" insults of our biological son, I knew that adopted kids don't have a monopoly on rejecting their parents, so none of this worried me.

I easily dismissed their concerns with all of the blind optimism of someone who had waited through four years of infertility for a baby and now finally thought she might get one. "Don't be surprised if you get placed quickly," our social worker told us. "Most adoptive parents aren't ready to be that open, and it's something a lot of birth mothers look for."

Our agency asked that each hopeful adoptive family put together what they called a profile and other adoption professionals sometimes call a "Dear Birth Mom" letter. (The reason they call it a profile, our agency explained, is that a pregnant woman considering adoption is not a birth mother; she is an expectant mother and should be respected as such.) When a woman came to the agency saying she was considering placing her child for adoption, they gathered at least five profiles to share with her. The profiles were pulled on the basis of any requirements that she might have. If a potential birth mother said she wanted an adoptive family where one parent was a teacher, only the teacher profiles would be pulled. If none of the profiles appealed to the woman, she could ask for more.

The profile contained information about us, about our

path to adoption and our intentions as adoptive parents. And the profiles are usually printed out on pretty paper.

"Pretty paper?" I asked Denise, our social worker, when she gave us the instructions.

"It matters," she said. "You'd be surprised."

It was a lot of pressure to take to the stationery store. My son and I spent a long time analyzing our choices. I rejected the pastel baby feet as too pushy, the blue sky and clouds as too ethereal. I finally decided on white with a tasteful abstract green border. We made a dozen copies and dropped them off at the agency.

While our agency allowed "matches" as early as the seventh month, they stressed to us that a match was nothing more than a woman expressing her right to consider an adoption plan. It was not the promise of a baby; it was not a guarantee that we would be parents again.

"There is always a fifty percent chance that a woman who chooses you will change her mind," Denise made clear. "A real baby changes things and no matter how sure she is while she's pregnant, she will need to make that decision again once she has the baby." It was a common refrain from the agency during our wait: "Guard your heart," they told us. "The baby isn't yours until the papers are signed."

Seven months after completing our adoption home study, our social worker called. "There's a woman who seems like a good fit for you, and we would like to share your profile with her."

Jessica was nineteen, they told us, and African-American. The birth father, who was choosing not to be involved, was white, like us. The baby was healthy—Jessica's prenatal care had been good. "And it says here what she's having," Denise added. "Do you want to know?"

We did. A girl, she told us, due April 4. A week later we got another call. Jessica wanted to meet with us.

Our agency facilitated our first meeting at a downtown restaurant. Jessica brought three of her closest friends, and we all sat across from one another, fidgeting awkwardly. Jessica was polite, guarded but not shy, and greeted us with sonogram pictures of the baby she was carrying. She was due in two months and feeling good.

I liked Jessica right away. I liked her confidence and sense of humor. I liked her wide smile. And I liked how direct she was with us. "I'm going to name the baby Madison," she told us. "You can change it later but that's the name I'm going to give her."

When it was time to go we exchanged phone numbers and last names. Over the next few weeks she and I talked regularly—not just about Madison but about other things too. Politics, music, Jessica's plans to travel and go to school. One day I hung up the phone after a particularly long conversation and told my husband, "If she decides not to place Madison, she'll be a good mother."

We talked about the adoption, too, about what her plans were and why she chose us to be part of it. It was clear to me that Jessica had made her decision thoughtfully and with attention to what she needed and wanted and what she believed her daughter needed too.

"You already had a son," she said. "I liked knowing Madison would have a brother. I also liked what you said about including me. And the paper. I liked your paper. It was tasteful."

At the first meeting at the restaurant, Jessica told us that she knew she would want to be alone with Madison for the three days before she could legally sign the surrender. We said we understood. But the morning that Madison was born she called to say that she had changed her mind and wanted us to come in.

"I need to see you with her," she said simply.

Even after we arrived home with Madison, I could not get Jessica's tears out of my mind. I felt numb. I didn't know how to answer when people congratulated us. They saw only the happy event, but each time Madison cried I felt sure that every one of her ordinary infant sorrows was magnified by the separation from her birth mother. This was not the gauzy, soft-focus motherhood I had envisioned.

Jessica was everywhere because she was in my daughter. The shape of her brown eyes, the curve of her face—they became mixed up in my mind. During every diaper change I'd gaze at Madison's small body and imagine how Jessica must have looked at one week old. They mirrored each other; the vulnerability of the mother who had given up her child and the child who had lost her mother. The similarities were so striking that I used to slip and call Madison by Jessica's name.

"You need to move on," friends said. "You need to let Jessica move on. Quit taking her phone calls. Step up and be Madison's mother!" But no one could tell me how to be her mother when she already had a mother. I could care for her—rock her, feed her, and sing her to sleep—but something would not allow me to claim her.

Was it the phone calls? Jessica called about once a week to hear how Madison was doing and to tell me what was going on in her life. I kept my stories sweet and lively. She was working hard to put her life back in order and was forthright with me about her struggles. She missed Madison, she told me. The decision was the right one but oh, she missed her. I welcomed our talks even as I shrank from them. I felt it was my duty to hear her cry. It was the least I could do, I thought, because I had her baby. My guilt was a necessary purgatory, an inadequate payment for my privilege.

Each time, I would hang up determined to embrace Madison as my own. Jessica wanted me to be Madison's mother, didn't she? She chose me. She signed the papers. She had released her to me, and now I was failing her trust.

So I went through the motions. I sang to Madison so she would learn my voice. I strapped her to me and walked in circles so she would learn the rhythm of my movements. I hoped proximity would breed devotion. But I felt like a liar when we went out and people said what a pretty baby I had. Not my baby, I wanted to tell them, anxious not to take Jessica's credit.

"She even looks like you!" some gushed. Of course this wasn't true. Her smooth coffee-with-cream skin is nothing like my own rosy complexion. Such was their strong determination to fit her to our family.

"She looks just like her birth mother," I'd reply. I wanted them to see Jessica, to acknowledge her. I couldn't stand to have her obliterated, even in casual conversation. It was as if they were trying to deny the truth of Madison, the fact of who she was beyond being my adoptive daughter. I didn't want to pretend that she came to us without her own history. But at the same time, polite society seemed to want to dismiss her origins. Per United States law, Madison's post-adoption birth certificate even listed me as the woman who gave birth to her.

The next time Jessica called, I tentatively told her how I was feeling. "I can't stop thinking about you and how hard this must be," I said, my voice cracking. "I know how sad you are. . . . "

"I don't want you to feel guilty," Jessica admonished me. "I want you to love her. I need you to love her and be happy."

"But how can I be happy when you're hurting so much?" I asked.

"It's easier when I think of you cherishing her," she said. "I need you to do that for her, and for me too. I don't regret this."

I wanted it to make better sense. We didn't find Madison languishing in a destitute orphanage. She didn't come to us with a history of abuse and neglect. I didn't know how to justify this great gift of her presence in our lives at the expense of her mother. If there were just something I could hang it on, an obvious reason that Madison was better off with us—but there wasn't. There was just the word of her first mother, who said, "This is what I need to do."

In my lowest moments, I would browse the list of adoptive parents on our agency's website. One night, I happened upon a profile of a fantastic family, African-American professionals who ran a newspaper and had a daughter the same age as my son. They should have gotten Madison, I thought. They were better educated than me, had better jobs—and could give Madison the one thing I never could: a connection to the black community.

My friend Elisabeth, who used to do patient support at an abortion clinic, took me to task.

"This is a choice issue," she told me. "You keep telling me how strong and smart Jessica is, but you're second-guessing her. That's not fair."

"I just want us to both be winners in this," I said.

"There is more than one way to be a winner here," she replied. "Stop denigrating Jessica's decision."

I had been picturing the two of us balanced on opposite sides of a tipping scale. If one of us was the real mother, then the other one was not. If one of us was happy, then the other must be sad. But when I hung up with Elisabeth, I realized that I couldn't ease Jessica's struggle by taking it on as my own. Besides, that's not what Jessica wanted; she did not want her sorrow to color these first months of Madison's life. It was my guilt that betrayed her, not my love for Madison.

When I stopped feeling so consumed by what Jessica had lost, I was able to find joy in what I gained, the everyday pleasures of parenting again—dressing my daughter, giving her a bath. Certainly, with that joy came vulnerability and the insecurity my worried friends predicted. Sometimes I don't want to share Madison. Sometimes I want to feel that I am the only mother she has and will ever need. But even at its most challenging, I still believe in openness. How much easier it will be for our daughter, I think, to never have to search for her roots. She will never have to wonder why her first mother chose adoption; she can ask her.

Jessica lives in our city and visits when her busy life allows, which ends up being about once a month, and we e-mail and phone more often. A few weeks ago she came over and made us jerk chicken with mango salsa; she is studying to be a chef. We joked that now we know where Madison gets her enthusiastic love of good food. After dinner I shared the beginnings of this essay with her and we cried a bit together.

"I didn't know it was so hard for you," she said.

"Well." I shrugged, helplessly. "I didn't know how to tell you."

Last summer Jessica and I took a trip to Washington State together so Madison could meet her extended birth family. Jessica was hoping, in part, to show them that it had all worked out okay and that her decision to place Madison with us was a good one. Since they were an interracial family already, the transracial aspect did not grieve them; it was the loss of this wondrous first grandchild to strangers. "When they see us together, how things are, they'll understand," Jessica assured me. Still, we were both nervous.

The family reunion took place at a country club on a beautiful cool summer evening. It was amazing to meet people who looked like Jessica and thus like Madison too. I kept my camera ready. Madison, open and sunny, charmed everyone, and several people took me aside to thank me for making the trip. "It's my pleasure," I said honestly.

"She looks like her mother," said someone admiringly, and I felt the discomfort the comment left in the room. "Yes,

she does," I rushed to say. "She has Jessica's beautiful smile."
And they were generous with me too. "Better ask your
mommy," said Jessica's father when Madison reached for
another slice of cake. Then he handed her to me, although I
know it pained him.

When the party spilled outdoors, Madison and Jessica
wandered away to play in one of the sand traps on the club's
golf course. I stood on the edge and snapped a series of
pictures—first Madison and Jessica crouching together to
poke at the sand. Then Madison with her head thrown back
to look up at Jessica while Jessica gazed down at her, smiling
with great tenderness. Then a shot of Madison laughing and
running away. Running toward me.

15.
Half the Work, All the Fun
Marc and Amy Vachon

On the outside, we are a typical family. A mother and father, with two children and a couple of cats, living under one roof in a middle-class suburb. We even have a white picket fence. Like most parents, our lives consist of school pickups and drop-offs, work commutes, playdates, and our children's swimming and music lessons. Nothing remarkable here.

But everyone has a life that goes deeper than appearances, and we are no different. Those who know us paint a more accurate picture of our family. They speak of us as their "fifty-fifty" friends, the ones devoted to a style of parenting and living that makes everything come out even between us. They laugh and good-naturedly rib us about our devotion to this idealistic vision. Some say we are an example of an egalitarian marriage—perhaps even role models for what feminism promised for the home but hasn't yet delivered. New acquaintances usually need an explanation of our lifestyle in order to understand how we operate, and we eagerly introduce what we call Equally Shared Parenting.

Many parents today can probably identify with this term. They would assume that we simply mean men doing their fair share around the house and with the kids, a scenario that is in fact quite common now. But we are talking about something beyond the involved dad married to the working mom—an arrangement that usually means an overworked woman who manages the home and a man who remains her understudy and the family's main provider. Equally Shared Parenting is our name for parents who are equals in both spirit and action. They own the depths of child raising to the same degree, they invest the same amount of energy and thought in managing their household, they uphold each other's careers as equivalent in value, and they nurture a balanced life above almost all other ideals. Neither partner directs the other; neither is the other's subordinate helper. Many question whether such a relationship actually exists. It does—and, for better or worse, we're living it every day.

Amy and I met on a cold evening in early spring after finding each other on a computer dating site. By then, we'd each had our share of bad dates, nonstarter relationships, and near misses. Amy had already been married and divorced, and I had never let the idea of settling down take hold. We were both in our late thirties, and had learned the art of cutting to the chase with prospective partners while still letting life unfold at its proper pace. On our first date, we shared the short version of our life stories, and then began to speak of more emotionally personal details. We discovered that we shared a similar dream for the future. We both wanted to connect with a peer—not a trophy partner or someone to relieve us from life's heavy lifting or menial tasks. Materially, we each felt we had come to terms with what "enough" was, and neither of us cared at this point about amassing additional financial wealth.

As we split the check, our discussion turned to the vision of an ideal coupled lifestyle—one in which both partners had full and balanced lives and wanted the best for each other, and one in which children were evenly shared, money was earned together, hobbies were preserved (within reason), and the home was truly a reflection of all inhabitants. The conversation was theoretical, of course, but we each felt inspired by this vision we had concocted together. That evening, as Amy told me later, she went home happy but wary that I wasn't what I seemed. And I knocked on my best friend's door to announce that I had finally met the woman I would marry. Exactly eighteen months later, we did just that.

And so we lived happily ever after, a perfect match of equality and balance. Um, not exactly. We actually moved in fits and starts toward our goals. In countless follow-up conversations to our first date, we sealed our commitment to build and grow our family as peers and preserve time for the things that mattered most to each of us. All around us were stories—from family, friends, coworkers, parenting books, and the media—describing how couples become anything *but* balanced and equal from the moment they hit parenthood. We were determined to be different, but didn't get much time to work out the details before our daughter was born ten months later. We were both working full-time and neither of us wanted to give up our career to be a stay-at-home parent. At the same time, we wanted to minimize the need for outside child care.

We decided to use my paternity leave benefit plus my accrued vacation time. That way, I could spend two days per week at home during Amy's maternity leave.

Right away we knew we were on to something good. The majority of our early days as parents were actually relaxing—unlike the pressure cookers described by many others—with all baby-focused activities shared between us. Amy was breast-feeding but also pumping milk for me to feed by bottle once a day. We experimented with the time of day to give the bottle in order to optimize sleep for each of us. We learned together how to change a diaper, soothe a crying baby, listen to a frustrated spouse, and function on reduced hours of sleep. We figured out how to be parents while still getting in daily showers and keeping up with the laundry. But we also knew it wouldn't last. Soon our time off would be over and we would have to find a new way of sharing parenting roles.

Amy's prospects for a reduced work schedule were buoyed by a female coworker who had transitioned into a four-day workweek with good results. As it turned out, the company was happy to keep Amy under the same arrangement. I, on the other hand, was offered a management position that came with additional responsibility. I didn't know any other coworkers—especially not men—working reduced hours. I decided to reject the management offer, ask for a cut in hours, and be prepared to look elsewhere if necessary. It sounds radical, but I had prepared myself by working part-time in my single, childless days. I was secure in my decision to prioritize a balanced life as a good reduced-hours worker over a high prestige job title with longer work hours. When male coworkers teased me, I simply reminded myself that everyone makes his or her own best choices.

As the saying goes, luck is the intersection of preparation and opportunity. We got lucky. My company decided to offer all twenty-two hundred employees a six-month sabbatical with no pay but full benefits in an attempt to avoid layoffs. We couldn't afford to forgo all pay, but I offered to reduce my salary and benefits commensurate with a permanent reduction in hours. My manager agreed, and the groundwork for our dream arrangement was in place. I would work Monday, Wednesday, and Friday and Amy would work Monday through Thursday—each about thirty hours per week. We would need outside child care for only two days per week. Neither of us would suffer a résumé gap brought on by childbirth. Our family would earn more money than if one of us were to stay home but less than if we both worked full-time. We happily invested in balanced lives and equal opportunities for a chance to share them with our child.

But as we were working out the details of our arrangement, another complication arose. During her maternity leave,

Amy voraciously read stacks of books on how to care for a child. She was up to speed on the latest in feeding options, sleep philosophies, safety concerns, educational toys, and outside child-care facilities. I was more of a laid-back parent, and believed I would figure it out along the way. I deferred to Amy's plans, structure, and schedule during her leave, and focused on the transition to reduced hours at work. As Amy began to dictate the when and how of naps, baths, and "tummy time," we realized we had veered off course. Amy owned all the child-care decisions and I had become the junior "helper" parent.

This imbalance threatened our plan for an equal relationship. The issue came to a head on the day Amy was to return to work. She was confident in her decision to return, leaving our daughter in my willing hands. The morning routine worked flawlessly, with two breast-feeds and one pumping session. What happened next is legendary in our house for cementing our journey toward Equally Shared Parenting. Amy thoughtfully and lovingly presented me with The List, her report on the proper care and feeding of our daughter for the next eight hours she would be with me. My response was cruel, but proved necessary. I ripped it up in front of Amy, announcing that I would get to run the show when I was the one at home. In that act, I renamed myself as an equal—a full parent rather than a day-care provider.

At the time, my bold action was unsettling to Amy on a day when she already felt vulnerable and anxious. For me, The List represented false equality. My rejection of Amy's instructions was a clear signal that we needed to walk the walk or risk abandoning our dream. This one incident set in motion weeks, if not months, of unraveling our expectations around gender roles in parenting. Here we were, two mature adults committed to equally sharing the raising of our child, but at times we were each hurt by how much the other didn't seem to understand. Amy felt unappreciated for her hard work and diligence orchestrating a plan for our daughter's care. I felt marginalized, and therefore less fulfilled, despite my commitment to be an equal partner. We didn't realize it at the time, but we were bumping right up against a cultural icon—the sacrosanct mother-child bond. We're taught that mothers *own* the care of their children, that mothers are better at it. And isn't it more efficient for the mother to make the rules and have the dad help out as needed?

We realized we would have to throw out a lot of cultural expectations and build our own way of parenting from scratch. Did we want to sterilize bottles? Would we use disposable or cloth diapers? Should we co-sleep or use a crib? What about pacifiers? We realized that in order to enjoy the fruits of parenting as absolute partners, we had to share not just the physical but also the mental work of parenting. This meant Amy had to abdicate ownership of our daughter's care to the team, I had to stand up for my ideas rather than take the easy way out by just adopting all of Amy's, and each of us had to make room for the other's parenting style.

The mental transition wasn't entirely easy. Like most women, Amy was conditioned to believe that caring for "her" baby was, well, her responsibility above all others. Her mother had done almost all the caretaking before her father died when Amy was eight, and she had no other role models.

It was a combination of fear and love that helped her let go. Fear that she would otherwise carry the vast responsibility of parenting alone, and love for her baby daughter and me— a duo that deserves just as much intimacy as our society awards mothers and babies.

With a renewed commitment to equal sharing, we opted for what was initially the much harder route, engineering *our* plan for raising a baby. We discussed and agreed on how to prepare our daughter's bottles, the basic sequence of events in her bedtime routine, and when to start solid foods. But we also left plenty of room for our own individual parenting styles. Amy left the house with a fully stocked diaper bag, for example, while I was comfortable traveling light— very light. When I found myself at the park without a needed spare diaper on my day at home, Amy was not allowed to comment. No rolling her eyes or pointing out that she would have been more prepared. The same was true when it was Amy's turn to venture out with our daughter. Our goal was not to teach our daughter that both her parents were the same, but rather that she was going to be cared for, nurtured, and loved by two different people who respected each other enough to let it happen. When our son was born three years later, we gave the same gift to him.

As it turns out, we have rather different parenting styles. Amy is a planner and I love spontaneity; we're fond of saying that Amy's job is to get us from A to B and my job is to make it interesting. There are days when we argue about how to care for our kids—whether they need an extra pair of sneakers, when to insist they wash their hands, if they have to hold our hands crossing every street. We struggle like all couples with one watching the other do something differently—and try not to instantly label the behavior as "wrong."

But we have come to appreciate each other's strategies and instincts for child care and learned volumes from each other about how to be far better parents than either of us alone could have been. We believe our strengths are enhanced and our neuroses diluted as our kids experience both the organized and by-the-book parenting approach of their mother and the more spontaneous and daring ways of their father. We each feel like a valued partner with authority and power to propose changes and solutions. No topic is off-limits for a healthy discussion, and there is enough wiggle room for both of our personalities.

As a result, I am not emasculated and Amy is not expected to know it all. It has been a hard-fought victory for our family, and we are inordinately proud of our determination. Our kids come to either of us for comfort at various times, often running past the other in the process. The jilted parent remembers that our parenting centers on our kids rather than how they can fulfill us as parents. The mother/child bond has become a mother-father-child triangle.

Unfortunately, just because we shared breadwinning and child raising equally did not mean the rest of our lives were equal yet. Our next frontier was housework. We had, and still have, different standards for household cleanliness. Amy feels her life is more in order when the house is clean— she feels lighter, happier, and more productive. I believe a superclean house is an undue burden that takes an inordinate amount of time from other activities. Somehow these differences didn't matter before we had kids. Back then, I did enough to prove to Amy that I wasn't a caveman when it came to work around the home, and Amy enjoyed her life instead of worrying about the house. But the added responsibilities, time commitments, and requisite "stuff" that come with having children bumped up against our habits.

Even though we each silently understood that more housework was required when our daughter was born, we didn't initially agree on who was going to do it. I felt that because I contributed more to the family than most men by downshifting my career and caring for the baby two days per week, I wasn't responsible for the additional housework. Amy pointed out that equality-in-full was part of the foundation upon which we agreed to build our relationship, and that this included housework. Once we laid the facts on the table, we both agreed that housework too needed to be equally shared, but that it could only be tackled as a team after we agreed on how clean *we* (rather than either of us alone) wanted our house to be. The battle was on for determining what this meant.

Of course, we both dug in our heels and defended unreasonable positions. I said things like "It's not important how clean our house is," and Amy demanded the house be prepared for an unannounced guest to be able to eat off the floor. The negotiation carried on intermittently for months. We declared a truce by breaking the most contentious tasks down, one by one, and coming to a mutually satisfactory way of handling them. What constitutes a clean kitchen? How often do the bedsheets need to be changed? What are the food staples to routinely check to see if they are stocked before either of us heads to the grocery store? The questions went on and on. It was an exercise that taught us a lot about ourselves and defined the ground rules for merging our ideals.

Assigning the tasks was actually easy once we agreed on the standards. We split some of them down the middle, such as cooking and laundry, and then each picked the remaining tasks that were least offensive to us. Many chore divisions came naturally as a result of which one of us was home on which days. The goal was near-equivalent time spent on housework each week by each of us. Paying bills, painting the bathroom, food shopping, grass cutting—all of it was included.

Truth be told, we come down along fairly typical gender lines in who does what, but the result is far from typical. We now proceed with completing our tasks at our own pace and in accordance with our joint standards. We have no need to nag each other, pretend to forget our responsibilities or to be incompetent to do a chore, silently resent each other for not pulling our weight, or assign each other "honey-do" tasks. We both have ownership in the running of the house and often spontaneously help each other as circumstances arise. We renegotiate as situations change, household projects are completed, or imbalances are noted. We mix things up on occasion so that we each gain competence in most areas of household maintenance. We're a team in our dedication, not adversaries trying to catch each other in an act of inequality. Appreciation is assumed and fully understood by both of us.

. . .

Once the housework pie was equitably divided, something magical happened. A sort of freedom opened up that is rare for parents with young children. We had time to pursue our own lives. Each of us was free to become involved in any hobby or passion that appealed to us—without the slightest hint of guilt. The house was running like a well-oiled machine and the payoff was plenty of time for grown-up fun. I bicycled to and from work and played tennis a couple of times per week. Amy played violin almost every weekend and walked to and from work most days. We enjoyed both dinners out with friends and date nights with each other.

Today, this magic continues to spill over to other areas of life. We are driven to make our job arrangements last and to please our employers by working hard and reducing inefficiencies at the office. Our kids get to see lots of us from the best angles—rejuvenated, active, and happy. We seldom yearn for a vacation *from* our lives. Instead, we are determined to enjoy these days to the fullest because we are keenly aware of our good fortune. And although we realize that some of our situation could be attributed to luck, much of it is the result of careful planning and tending. The foundations upon which we've built our lives are not dependent on the way the wind blows. Our lifestyle feels sustainable well beyond the typical retirement age.

To our kids, the week is divided into Mommy days, Daddy days, and family days. It's normal for them to remind us whose turn it is to put which of them to bed each night, who's home with them on which day, who gets to pick them up on school days. But the world doesn't always see our lifestyle as ordinary. We have to train people to connect with both of us equally—the pediatrician who now knows that I will show up for appointments as often as Amy, the teacher of a children's music class who at first addressed only Amy, the preschool director who now calls upon me to give recommendations to new parents considering the school. When first learning of our arrangement, these outsiders stroke my ego admiringly and tell Amy how lucky she is, but they catch on quickly that this is not how we want to be treated. Stereotypical gender roles run deep, we know, and we can't control first impressions.

Why aren't more couples living like us? Some have no interest—and that is fine. Most adults grow up believing that all people are equal, but make choices that send them down traditional paths instead. Men hold on to their primary-breadwinner mentality, thinking that anything else is an abdication of duty. Or they shun "feminine" caretaking roles, opting instead for fully absorbing careers. Women, too, push themselves into inequality by holding fast to their status as ruler of the home and primary parent. And so traditional ways live on, even after feminism made so much possible.

There may be another reason egalitarian marriages such as ours are still uncommon. It may have something to do with the sacrifices required—sacrifices that we feel are outweighed by the rewards of intimacy, peace, fun, and purposefully present living. Parents who make the decision to become equals have to devote themselves to a life of continuous communication. They cannot take the easy way out and silo their expertise in breadwinning, housework, or child raising; they must be experts at all three and operate from a joint mission statement. Neither parent can channel full energies into a power career that upsets the division of labor at home or with the kids, nor can either parent check out of paid work. In the long run, an equal family may garner less money because both parents peak in moderate careers with moderate incomes. Each of these sacrifices has a flip-side benefit, but they illustrate how Equally Shared Parenting goes against the grain of standard thinking.

What about how our choices will affect our children? As in any family, the personalities and arrangements of parents have profound effects on their children, and we're engaged in a small-scale experiment with large-scale consequences for two budding humans. Our hope is that our balanced lives can model for them that adulthood can be fun and fulfilling—not unending drudgery and sacrifice—and that success is not defined only by worldly accomplishment. We expect our equality will show them that women and men are equals at work and at home—and should be treated as such. That either gender can drive when we're all in the car. That both parents are capable of knowing their school friends' names and addresses. And we believe that giving our kids large doses of both of their parents will teach them two unique ways of dealing with the highs and lows of everyday life.

. . .

To passersby, we are just a mainstream family living the standard American dream. But we've reworked that dream ever so slightly on the surface, and created a seismic internal shift. Inside our average-looking home are two part-time workers with equally important careers who place high value on both the paid and unpaid labor required to run a household. We've replaced gatekeeping any facet of our home with the shared plan of the team. We've transferred the physical and mental ownership of child rearing and homemaking from one parent to both. By giving up the push for the corner office, the vacation home at the beach, or early retirement in Florida, we've made room for the moderate here-and-now and intimate lives with our kids and each other. Where there was stress there is now balance. Where there were separate spheres there is now full partnership. Where there was the promise of worldly riches there is now the peace of "enough." Where there was social power there is now everyday enjoyment. Our kids are normal, happy children who don't know much about how their family might differ from others. Our daughter has just finished kindergarten and has grown from a somewhat shy toddler to an outgoing and confident young person in her own right. Our son is a social and extremely verbal three-year-old who keeps us hopping.

Of course, we don't have this thing all wrapped up yet. We're still learning every day, adjusting and tweaking and doggedly talking things out. So much lies ahead of us that we don't yet know how to share equally—homework help, our kids' sports and after-school activities, the dreaded teenage years, college preparation and financing, our own parents' aging, and myriad genuine crises and challenges.

For now we look forward to these next phases, with faith in our vision and a plan to have fun along the way.

16.
How Homeschooling Made Our Family More of What We Wanted It to Be **Paula Penn-Nabrit**

Let's start at the beginning. My husband, C (his name is Charles, but so is our eldest twin, so C is easy, plus that's what his mother calls him), and I came to homeschooling by default. I wish we could say we planned this, oh so carefully, but that would be a lie. In the same vein, I wish I could say we all loved the process of homeschooling. But unlike many homeschooling families, ours did *not* love it, at least not while we were doing it. My husband and I were often tired and discouraged, and whether they actually meant it or not, our kids told us they hated being homeschooled—and they told us every day.

Unlike many new parents, not only did my husband and I not know we would homeschool, I'm not even certain we had heard of homeschooling outside the context of nineteenth-century history. Our in-depth analysis of educational options began in 1983 when the twins were three years old. It was pretty much limited to the traditional triumvirate of public school, parochial school, or private school. Period. Back then, charter schools didn't exist, nobody was talking about vouchers, online learning happened only inside multinational corporations, and as I said, we thought homeschooling, with the possible exceptions of missionaries, Mennonites, and the Amish, ended with the pioneers and other purveyors of Manifest Destiny. We were not part of the progressive and informed parent party.

But educational ignorance notwithstanding, there were some things we knew right at the beginning, unequivocally and beyond the shadow of a doubt. We knew we loved Charles, Damon, and Evan abundantly and beyond measure. We knew they were each unique and fascinating children. We didn't concern ourselves with the question of what they would become quantitatively. We weren't interested in whether they would become doctors or lawyers or engineers. We were interested in the qualitative; we wanted them to become healthy, conscious, and contributing members of the world's community. We knew we really, truly enjoyed their company. We knew they deserved a holistic and well-balanced launch into the universe. We knew we were responsible for doing our best to ensure that they received it. And as a corollary to all of the above, we knew we wanted to be a fully functional family, not just a bunch of people who shared some genetic material and a mailing address.

In retrospect, I'm certain some of the stuff we knew seemed so exquisitely intense and illuminated to us because we had such a difficult time having children. We suffered two miscarriages before we had the twins, Charles and Damon. The pregnancy with them required almost six months of strict bed rest. We then suffered two more miscarriages before we had Evan. And his gestation was not without its own nail-biting aspects, as I contracted pneumonia during pregnancy. Ultimately, the difficulties converged with the successes and created an abiding sense of intense gratitude. We were so consciously aware and thankful that God had (finally) blessed us with strong, healthy kids that embracing a sense of obligation for good stewardship with them felt easy.

So, excited and filled with our own sense of wonder about them, we gleefully sent Charles and Damon and then Evan off to school "in due season." Had we been thinking rather than emoting, we probably could have anticipated the clash between our expectations and the inevitable realities of institutional education. We thought our kids' excitement and enthusiasm about learning, their admittedly incessant questioning of everything, and their urgency to know would be welcome and encouraged qualities. We thought our delight in their self-confidence would be shared with the adults they encountered. We were wrong, and for reasons we honestly never considered in advance: we thought of Charles, Damon, and Evan primarily as bright kids, not as black kids who happened to be bright. But boy, oh boy, there's nothing like immersion into the mainstream to clarify the gulf between what you think about your kid and what the world of institutionalized education thinks about him.

At first we thought the "problem" was public school. There was the whole slightly larger than you'd like student-to-teacher ratio; the ever-increasing pressure on teachers to do everything, leading too often to less than enthusiastic teaching; and, of course, the abiding guilt many prep school alums have if they send their own kids to public school. After all, if your parents sacrificed to send you to private school, the presumption is that you will make the same sacrifices for your own children. While our parents and grandparents were sympathetic and were always there with a listening ear and solid support, the situation they had faced was so different. C and I attended school in the sixties, when everything was in turmoil. He went to legally segregated schools in Memphis until tenth grade, when his family moved to Toledo. And while I attended integrated schools, it was still a turbulent environment. Our sons entered school in 1984, not 1954 or 1964 or even 1974. But it still seemed that at every turn we were surprised or shocked at yet another of our miscalculations about another teacher at yet another school. *Brown v. Board of Education* notwithstanding, we quickly learned the depth of truth in the adage that the more things change, the more they stay the same. (As an aside, there was a certain irony in the fact that C's uncle, the late James M. Nabrit, actually argued *Brown* before the United States Supreme Court with the late Thurgood Marshall.)

C and I initially processed the typical collection of "racial encounters" during the first few years of our kids' schooling within the matrix of class conflict, namely middle-class white women teachers who seemed uncomfortable with black children who weren't from dysfunctional families or a lower socioeconomic group. There is something potentially dangerous in the lure of helping "the less fortunate," something that frames the helper as a savior there to ennoble the less fortunate, and that danger is there for everyone in the helping professions, including teachers.

The challenge for our sons' teachers seemed to be the fact that they couldn't figure out how to "help" our sons and so classified them as arrogant and unmanageable. Example: Charles, who was a chatterbox in kindergarten, was talking during practice for the Hanukkah portion of the holiday program. When his teacher yelled at him for not paying attention and not understanding the importance of Hanukkah, he responded by telling her he knew the Messiah had already come. Like most children brought up in Apostolic, Pentecostal families like ours, Charles and his brothers began learning about Judaism and the Old and New Testaments of the Bible while still young fans of *Sesame Street*. He just wasn't yet intellectually mature enough to comfortably balance "competing" religious truths. But his teacher was even less mature. Her response was to slap him in front of the class. This was one of our first "incidents" in public school in Jacksonville, Florida.

We felt Charles needed to be corrected for talking, for not paying attention, and for thinking his religious beliefs excused him from respecting the beliefs of others. But we felt his teacher's response was an extremely irrational and totally unacceptable reaction to a four-year-old. And since we provided a clear and written prohibition against all forms of corporal punishment at enrollment, we were stunned and angry. An added complication was the fact that Damon had been telling us for months that "the teacher hates Charles."

The boys were in separate classrooms—at the school's insistence—and Damon's teacher indulged his periodic need to go "look in" on Charles. But as Charles never complained, and I hadn't observed anything troubling during my weekly visits as a room mother, we thought Damon just missed his brother. As it turned out, we were wrong. The teacher's explanation, corroborated by the principal, was that Charles was "the most arrogant and obnoxious person I have ever met."

We were stunned, especially after the principal told us both Charles and Damon were very conceited and too competitive. Their dad's response was very loud and fearfully simple: a) the boys were to finish out the year; b) the teachers were to pretend that they found them to be delightful; c) if any further violence occurred he promised to escalate it, directly and personally, on the responsible adult. As we left both women in tears I was busy thinking of how soon I could schedule an appointment with a child psychiatrist. C thought that was absurd; he figured if the kids were nuts we wouldn't need a couple of crazy white women to tell us. I wanted to believe him, but I wasn't (yet) that confident in my own abilities as a parent, especially as I had so completely dismissed Damon's observations. As soon as we got home I apologized to him and promised never to dismiss his feelings again—and I haven't. But I was equally unnerved by Charles's silence about what was happening in school. I pulled him onto my lap and told him that school was important, but not more important than him, and that Mommy and Daddy needed to know if anybody was ever mean to him because that was not allowed. Charles very calmly told me his teacher yelled at him a lot when I wasn't there. When I asked him what he did, he said, "When she starts yelling at me I just suck my thumb and look for Damon because I can't help her." While I was amazed at his coping skills, I was also ashamed that I hadn't been asking the right questions earlier.

I scheduled an appointment with one of the most respected child psychiatrists in town. In the spirit of full and fair disclosure, he told us he was quite familiar with the school and its excellent reputation and felt that the kind of racial bias I suspected was indeed quite rare within the ranks of professional educators. We appreciated his candor (or at least I did) and so we paid our money and proceeded with the process. Over the next several weeks he examined both boys, individually and together, observed them both in his office and at school, and spoke with their teachers and the principal. His final recommendation resonated with C specifically: "Get the boys out of that school ASAP!"

We figured if public school didn't work, no problem, there were other options, we'd try private school. Private school appealed to us in a number of ways. The class sizes were smaller, the curriculum was more intense, the instruction seemed more focused, and the facilities were flawless. Plus, by this point we were ready to relocate back to Columbus and I felt things would be better once we left the South. But with regard to our children's holistic development, private school was not better, just different. Here we had another set of "challenges" to add to the old ones. We still felt that Charles and Damon's teachers weren't sure how to react to two smart, confident black children. There were almost no other black kids—and absolutely no black teachers. The lack of black teachers was something we were able to handle. Our sons had a dad, two granddads, two uncles, a godfather, a pastor, and an assistant pastor, all strong black men, so the absence of black adult males at the school in any position other than janitorial was something we wished we could have avoided, but not a deal breaker because we could address it easily and openly with the boys. What we had a harder time with was our sense that the school was running contrary to the values we were trying to instill at home. The values issue was more complex, because social conduct and morality require personal discipline. We often felt as if the school was providing a kind of acceptable "out" facilitated by the dangerous belief that money creates more than economic privilege.

Conflicts over values aren't racially segregated and are often insidious, so we tried to be vigilant, having learned the hard way how completely clueless we could be about what was going on with our own kids. While we adored them, we knew our "little darlings" were far from perfect. Like many bright children, Charles, Damon, and Evan weren't always especially tolerant or understanding of kids with fewer abilities. C and I were intent on helping our kids understand that intellectual ability, or more specifically academic aptitude, is but one element of what it is to be fully human. We didn't want them to be academic snobs, unable (or unwilling) to interact comfortably with people regardless of their educational achievement or lack thereof.

Further, C has very distinct rules about good manners evidenced through speech. Profanity and disrespectful language are absolutely forbidden in our family. C never yelled at the children and consciously spoke to them respectfully, and he expected them to model that with others and especially with one another. I completely concurred (although it was more of a struggle for me), and since our kids had never experienced anything else at home, that's how they engaged people. And while C felt there could be instances in which fighting might be acceptable, he made it abundantly clear that he would never, ever tolerate teasing or bullying.

In a similar way, our family rule was that each of the boys could have a birthday party, every year if they wanted, but at each party, every boy in the class would be invited. Birthdays were not to be used as opportunities to make other children feel "less than."

We were unprepared for the challenges those simple social values presented in school. I was surprised at how often the same little boys were not invited to birthday parties openly discussed at school, and how embarrassingly grateful their mothers were when their sons were invited to our kids' parties. I couldn't believe the seeming callousness of the moms of the kids having those parties. I was shocked when Charles and Damon told me their English teacher used, as they phrased it, "the D word" in class. This was one of their earliest experiences with a male teacher and they were pretty excited about this guy, as he was fairly young and presumably "cool." Our sons were clearly confused by the obvious contradiction between what they had been taught at home and what they were hearing from a teacher. I didn't see anything cool about a middle school teacher using profanity in class and fully expected the teacher to apologize and at least pretend to be sincere about it. Imagine my surprise when he explained that that was the way boys and men talk to one another. Now imagine his surprise when I explained that we wouldn't accept his use of profanity in class with our sons and that if it happened again I'd let their father discuss it with him.

When their math teacher returned tests in declining grade order she too seemed surprised when I told her how upset Charles and Damon were. She felt that as each received an A they shouldn't have been concerned; further, she felt public humiliation was a good form of motivation. We began to feel that each of these instances collectively wore down the lessons about social responsibility we were trying to teach our sons at home.

But the issues of racial diversity and our conflicting value systems weren't our only challenges. On top of everything else, we simply couldn't afford private school, so we were perpetually on edge *and* broke.

It's one thing to be broke, to wake up in the middle of the night in a cold sweat wondering how you're going to pay the tuition bill. But that moment of panic should be assuaged by the calming and self-validating knowledge that you are providing your children with the absolute best education money can buy. That awareness is supposed to lull you back into some semblance of restful slumber for the remainder of the night. Then you get up the next morning renewed and refreshed with a revitalized burst of energy to "go make that money!" But it wasn't like that for us; when we woke up in a debt-induced cold sweat, our thoughts were gut-gnawing questions: Is this environment causing irreparable psychological harm? Are our children destined to join the ranks of successful black folks with great credentials but no sense of cultural or collective identity? How much adaptation and assimilation can occur before one loses one's sense of identity and becomes alienated from the self? Ultimately we would drift back to fitful sleep, broke *and* worried about the kind of men our sons would become.

So we spent the next few years doing what lots of parents do, namely monitoring and critiquing interspersed with confrontation and appeasement, plus hour upon hour upon hour of field trips, bake sales, book fairs, classroom parties, and regular discussions about the bill. But in the final analysis, we just couldn't make it work. In September of what turned out to be the boys' last year in school, I hosted a picnic for all the black families. I thought it would be helpful for all our sons to have a stronger sense of collective affinity at the school. The picnic was seen as a school event—one that I hadn't cleared with the administration—and that transgression, combined with the boys' tuition being late (again), resulted in them being unceremoniously expelled. To be certain we understood just how serious the school was about the expulsion, we were told that if we tried to send the boys, the school would "embarrass" them.

It was a painful yet brilliantly clarifying moment—it's how we came to homeschooling, and it's also how we began consciously formulating and stamping our own brand on ourselves as a unique collective, a functional family.

We had wanted to believe the problems we were having were isolated incidents, yet over time it became clear that the disconnect was between what we wanted, expected, and required for our sons and what any existing school system or individual school was able or willing to provide. Our parents and grandparents had the consolation of being pioneers and opening the doors of integrated education for their children. And because it was so new, certain pitfalls were inevitable and part of the challenge. But for C and me none of this was new. In fact, it was the very repetitive nature of the challenges that made them so distasteful. We were essentially going over the same ground and explaining the same kinds of things our parents and grandparents had covered decades earlier. We felt we were stagnating even as we followed the example set before us.

Our parents and grandparents adapted, adjusted, and outwitted the status quo because they believed that was necessary to provide the best for their children. But finally, C and I simply lost interest in the status quo. We didn't lose interest in the goal of providing the best for our kids; we just lost interest in the whole adaptation, adjustment, and assimilation part. After you do all that adapting and adjusting, what you're left with, having penetrated the status quo, didn't seem to be worth it or in the best interest of our kids. Proving we could do it, encouraging our children to rise above it, holding the moral high ground, setting an example, perfecting the "exceptional Negro" role—none of that held nearly the allure of simply doing the entire educational thing ourselves.

So after the boys were expelled, we decided that instead of continuing to critique the extant educational system, we would create our own. One of the first reading assignments we gave them was Stephen Biko's insightful essay on black consciousness, "I Write What I Like," even though they were just eleven and nine years old. C and I had read it years before, but it took on a new patina of urgency and encouraged us to think and talk, in very specific, concrete terms, about what kind of family we wanted to be, not just how we wanted to educate our kids. It was through this process of independent creation rather than adaptation, adjustment, or complaint that we began to make ourselves more of what we wanted to be.

That first conscious step of creating our own educational environment was helped by our nonparenting-related work. My husband and I have been self-employed for many years; in fact, I began our company in 1986 and since about 1990 we, like most entrepreneurs, basically eat what we can hunt and kill. There is no payroll check every two weeks, so we're pretty serious about our work. And a big part of that work is demographic research in which we collect information on immigration, employment, and education trends and break it down by race, gender, and national origin. Because of our work, we were well aware that with the exception of athletics, most black boys are consistently at the bottom of every measurement standard. We also knew that that statistical fact is deemed inelastic, meaning whether the parents were married or unmarried, college educated or high school dropouts, whether the kids went to public, private, or parochial schools or whether those schools were in urban, suburban, or rural communities, none of it affected the outcome. Black boys almost always finish last.

Some variation of that statistical reality is fairly well known, yet the explanation or the "why" of it is extremely polarizing. In public discourse, the why seems centered on one of two assumptions. One assumption says this inelastic statistic proves the inherent inferiority of African-American male children and the corresponding lack of regard for education in the African-American community. It would appear that there is no single ethnic or racial group on the planet, or certainly within the United States, with the depth of degradation, despair, and outright dysfunction as black Americans. If you didn't know better, you might even believe this nation's entire cultural, political, and economic decline is due to "the Negro problem." Given that view, it would follow that African-American male children would consistently hit the bottom of all academic measurement standards.

The other, equally polarizing assumption says the same inelastic statistic proves the existence of a conspiracy to destroy black boys, a conspiracy masterminded and implemented by the roughly 83 percent of classroom teachers in grades K-12 who are Caucasian women. This theory says that the single obstacle to the achievement of African-American boys is the white women who run educational institutions. From this worldview, one sees white women as so powerful and persuasive that they neutralize any and all positive messages of encouragement coming from parents, family, and the larger community.

While I am among the first to concede that provocative assumptions, polarizing views, and conspiracy theories are ideal as conversation stimulants, especially when presented collectively, they do absolutely nothing to help craft workable solutions. C and I decided to step away from the emotional energy bound up in both theories and engage in, dare I say it, a paradigm shift. It wasn't that we were bored with the theories of condemnation or conspiracy as much as we just couldn't afford the time to pursue either one. We had three boys who needed to learn and we needed to find answers. We were okay with the idea that there could be multiple answers, including some as yet untried.

We decided to rationally examine education as a process and identify opportunities for what is called in manufacturing "continuous process improvement." If you're making cars and all the blue ones are missing the fourth wheel, the thing to do is to examine the manufacturing process. It would be absurd to assume that (a) blue cars are somehow inherently inferior or (b) the assembly line workers are consciously conspiring against blue cars. Granted, either a or b is possible, but neither is probable. What is more likely is that there is an unidentified design flaw in the process, and all available energy should be focused on the identification and eradication of that flaw; that's process improvement. Based on this theory, C and I began to examine our educational ideal. We moved from affixing blame for the problem to identifying alternative solutions to fixing the problem itself. This was the next step in the process of homeschooling making us more of what we wanted to be. Rather than fight the power, we decided to begin flexing and exercising our own.

C and I began to question precisely what we wanted for our sons at our deepest level of analysis. Not surprisingly, this was far more challenging than pointing out what was wrong with every school the boys had attended. We knew the answers to the question of what we wanted for our sons would start us on the path of improved process design. After prayer and discussion, we came to the conclusion that we wanted Charles, Damon, and Evan to be fully committed to discovering and becoming who they were intended to be in the world. Now, as wacky and esoteric as that might sound, we knew it meant at a baseline level that they would have to come to conscious awareness of themselves as part of God's creation.

We concluded that if we worked to create an environment where they would be validated and nurtured spiritually, intellectually, and physically, academic achievement would happen as a foregone conclusion. We began to realize at a deep, conscious level that it is in the nature of humans to seek knowledge and that when that seeking, that desire to know and understand, diminishes, it is usually the result of blockage by external stimuli. Much of the defensiveness and finger pointing about the blockage is a pointless distraction because the removal of the blockage is more important than where it came from or whether its presence is intentional.

We focused our energy on removing all barriers to growth, and determined our primary objective was to create and maintain an environment where the search for knowledge of the Creator, knowledge of the universe, and knowledge of the self would be the dominant theme, not how many math problems can be completed in thirty minutes.

With that admittedly esoteric hypothesis in place, we moved to the quantitative aspect of crafting a curriculum. Here we began simply with the desire to allow Charles, Damon, and Evan to have some choices when the time came to decide about their future, especially college. We figured if we developed a curriculum challenging and comprehensive enough for Ivy League admissions, they would be assured of some choices. What we didn't want was for them to get to that point and find themselves essentially locked out of what they wanted to do because of our lack of forethought and preparation. The focus on future choices led to the relatively easy task of deciding on a core curriculum.

Ultimately, Charles and Damon attended Princeton and Evan went to Amherst. In our family the process of reentry into the arena of institutionalized education after home-schooling was intense. Fortunately, in each instance Charles, Damon, and Evan survived, strong and intact, with a clear sense of purpose in the world. So now they're adults, but some things haven't changed. There are some things we still know, unequivocally and beyond the shadow of a doubt. We know we love Charles, Damon, and Evan abundantly and beyond measure. We know they are each unique and fascinating people. We still aren't concerned with the question of what they will become quantitatively, and we still aren't interested in whether they become doctors or lawyers or engineers. We're still interested in the qualitative, and we are delighted they have become healthy, conscious, and contributing members of the world's community. We know we still really, truly enjoy their company. We know they deserved a holistic, well-balanced launch into the universe, and we are happy we were able to help them receive it. And as a corollary to all of the above, I can attest that homeschooling helped us become what we always wanted to be, a fully functional family, not just a bunch of people who share some genetic material.

17.

Till Life Do Us Part Meredith Maran

2006

"I'm leaving David," my friend Joanne tells me. She leans across the café table, white-knuckling a steaming mug of gunpowder tea. "I told him to be out of the house by next week."

I put my latte down a little too hard. Foamy milk streams down the sides of the glass. "Don't do it," I say.

Joanne stares at me, slack-jawed. I've just violated every feminist friendship's unspoken, incontrovertible rules: 1) Never offer advice unless asked—maybe not even then; 2) Never oppose a plan of action already set into motion; 3) Above all, never expect a friend to stay in a relationship that she, her friends, and/or her team of mental health professionals have determined to be unworkable, unhappy, oppressive, or— goddess forbid—all three. Especially a relationship in which there is a man.

"How can you *say* that?" Joanne says. "You know how unhappy I've been."

She's right. I do.

"Were you not *listening* when I told you how narcissistic

and passive-aggressive David is? That he asked me where the *diapers* are? That we haven't had sex in months?" Joanne recites her list of marital atrocities in a practiced rush. "Do you not *remember* how many times he's lost my keys? Taken the baby to the park without sunscreen? Made plans without asking me?"

Of course I remember. How could I forget all the times, since she married David three years ago, that the once unfailingly punctual Joanne has come to meet me late or not at all—because she couldn't find her keys, because she couldn't trust David alone with the baby, because she had to have it out with him before she could leave the house?

"But the two of you have a son together," I say. "Isn't that more important than your *keys*?"

Joanne glares at me as if she's never seen me before—or wishes she hadn't. After ten years of friendship, we're suddenly in the middle of our biggest fight. "What do you expect me to do, exactly?" she says. "Spend the rest of my life in an unhappy marriage? Raise my son in a house full of anger and blame?"

What *do* I think she should do? I ask myself. What do I wish I had done twenty-five years ago, when I made the very decision that I'm trying to keep Joanne from making now?

Stay with the father of your child, I want to tell her. Forgive his transgressions. Remember the reasons you married him. Live with him as happily ever after as you can.

What would I have done twenty-five years ago, if someone had said that to me? Incredible but true: our families, friends, and therapists watched my husband and me carve up our home, hearts, and kids without offering that advice.

And no wonder: Joanne can't be happy with the father of

her child, any more than I could have been happy with the father of mine. She doesn't love him anymore; she might even hate him, just as I stopped loving my husband the day I realized that loving him would no longer do any of us any good. Cleaving a family, committing this crime against nature, requires a mother—required *me*—to exist in two states of being at once: denial of its consequences, and raging with the kind of certainty that only anger supplies. Compassion, grief, remorse, sorrow—none had the power to propel me where I needed to go: *away.*

"It's better for the baby this way," Joanne says. "He'll still have both of his parents. He'll see that he has choices in his life, that no one has to stay stuck in an unhappy place."

"That's what I told myself when I left my kids' father," I say. "But now I know: the only person the divorce was better for was *me.*"

"You sound like a Republican," Joanne tells me—me, of all people: a lifelong radical with an FBI file as thick as my thigh.

She's right, I think. *She's wrong.*

"You don't have to be a Republican to see how much damage divorce does," I say. "You just have to be a mother who's done it to her kids."

One month later, Joanne files for divorce.

We haven't spoken since.

1968–1970

"You guys should get a divorce," I tell my parents. I take a long swallow of sangria, push my bowl of *chile verde* aside, and fix my gaze on one of them, then the other.

My father's face turns the color of *chile rojo*. My mother stabs her sopaipilla with her fork. They're just in from London, their first visitation to the Taos mountaintop where I live with my boyfriend, our two Nubian goats, and our small motley crew of friends. Mortified by our brown-rice-and-marijuana diet, my parents have taken my boyfriend and me out for a restaurant dinner, determined to feed us a "normal" meal. Which has turned out to be something other than normal.

"You don't love each other," I inform them. "It would have been better for all of us if you'd split up years ago." I have vested myself with the moral authority to deliver this truth. Someone has to, and who better than I? Until I ran away to escape it, I did sixteen years of hard time in the Upper East Side gulag of my parents' tight-lipped, clenched-jaw antipathy. Since childhood I've kept a list in my head of their hypocrisies and hostilities, a critical compendium, a parenting how-not-to. My life at age eighteen is a shining renunciation of my parents' deathly compromise, a model of unmarried bliss. After all, I'd lived with my boyfriend in vivacious (if occasionally contentious) nonmonogamy for four whole years.

"There's still hope for you," I assure my parents, speaking sympathetically, as if to foreigners or mentally deficient adults (in my eyes, of course, they are both). "It's true. You're old." (*Twenty years younger than I am at this writing, I feel compelled to interject.*) "But if you get a divorce now, you still have a few years left to find true love." Demonstrating the sexual and emotional riches that could be theirs, if only they would dare to claim them, my boyfriend runs his deerskin moccasin teasingly up the inside seam of my 501s, licks my earlobe, laces his Hopi ring–encrusted fingers sexily through mine.

My mother turns her head, as if from a crime scene. My father leaves the table so fast, his chair crashes to the floor.

Two years later, my parents send a telegram to the Berkeley house I share with my new boyfriend, asking me to give them a call. I dial their London number from the pay phone on the corner, having first billed the call to Gulf Oil.

My parents tell me they're getting a divorce. I burst into tears.

1972–1983

"Before we get started, there's one thing I need to know." The couples counselor looks from one end of her white Haitian cotton couch to the other, from my husband to me. "Are you here for marriage counseling," she asks, "or are you here to talk about divorce?"

"I want us to make our marriage work," my husband says.

"There's nothing we can do to make this work," I say at precisely the same time. My husband and I gaze at each other through a blurry long white Haitian cotton tunnel of tears.

"We have two *kids*," my husband says. As if this is something I don't know; as if this is something we haven't said—*sobbed*—to each other a hundred—*a million*—times. As if I don't know that I'm doing the very thing I promised myself I'd never do ten years ago, when I married this carefully chosen man in the Oakland apartment we'd shared, by then, for a year.

"I don't want to do this to our kids," I say. "I don't want to do this to *us*. But we've already tried everything there is to try." Not even my grieving husband can dispute that this is true. In the past four years since his mother suddenly died, our second child was born, and the activist organization that held us together fell apart, my husband and I have spent our kids' college funds, and then some, on every kind of therapy there is. We've learned to speak in *I* messages, to listen actively. We've taken romantic intimacy-building vacations and separate autonomy-building retreats. We've dutifully performed our therapist's homework assignments: had nonverbal conversations, nonsexual touching, noninvasive sex. We bought a king-size waterbed, built it into a bay window in our bedroom, and surrounded it with a dozen scented candles. But even sleeping with our heads in the clouds hasn't kept us from rolling away from each other in the night.

"I want a divorce," I say. The biggest truth I've ever told. *The biggest lie.*

1984–1996

I do it again.

I fall in love, and it goes bad, and I stay as long as I can— *longer.*

I stay twelve years. I stay until she leaves me.

I stay because I tell myself every day that it will get better, that I can make it better, that we both want so badly to make it better, how could it not get better—tomorrow if not today. I stay because it's a woman I'm having problems with this time, and women are so good at *processing,* so good at *working our issues out.* Aren't we? I stay because therapists will see us five days a week, and between us we are keeping three of them in *New Yorker* subscriptions and Kleenex, so we are only on our own, with our screaming fights and our heaving sobs, on weekends, federal holidays, and the month of August. I stay because I do love her and she does love me. My solar plexus aches for her. My DNA howls, I swear it does, when I think of us being apart.

(Is that love? Or illness? Is there a difference? How would I know?)

I stay because there is always something else to try: active listening, romantic vacations, king-size beds. *But wait. Haven't I tried those things before?*

I stay because she is something like a parent to my children, and I will not put them—*my six-foot-tall sons, my men, my little boys*—through another divorce.

Soon after she leaves me, my eighteen-year-old son takes up residence on another continent.

My sixteen-year-old spends the next few years in and out of Juvenile Hall.

1996–Forever

I do it again.

And this time, it is good.

It is so good that despite having been, when I met my beloved, battle-scarred, battle-scared; charred to a bitter crisp by twelve years of scorched-earth love—in the ten years that I have known this goodness I have not questioned, or analyzed, or overthrown how good it is.

It is so good that I—I, who meant forever when I said it, *or thought I did,* and then didn't, and never forgave myself for not really meaning it (*but I did, when I said it*); I, who will go to my grave asking myself *what is family, then, if it couldn't be what I so badly wanted it to be*—know better than to try and twist this love into my own, or anyone's, shape-shifting notion of *how it's supposed to be.* Yes, I want her to love my children. I want my children to love her. But even after ten years with me she is something of a stranger to my sons, who once lived inside me, where she lives now. Despite this, to some extent, they do. We do. *We all manage to love one another.* In our own family way.

On my good days, I find this liberating: I cannot pretend that this love is for anyone's benefit but mine. Certainly it is not for my sons, who are old enough, now, to feel relieved that their mother is taken care of, not alone: not theirs to own anymore, but not theirs to worry about, either. They are almost old enough to rejoice in their mother's happiness. But they will never be old enough to stop wanting what they will never have, their mother and their father with them together, the four of us swimming side by side in the one river of our blood.

On my bad days I find this loss—theirs, his, mine—a greater sadness than I can bear.

On most days I feel the joy that beats inside my sadness,

and the sadness that beats inside my joy. Why was it not until I'd finished having children, until I was halfway through my life, that I found the love that will last forever? Precisely because I was finished having children. Precisely because I was halfway through my life.

(*Having children together, my lover says, is the one thing that is missing from what we have. But what a big thing that is, I say worriedly; the biggest thing there is. And this is how good it is: when I ask how she can forgive me for depriving her of this biggest of all big things, she says, and I believe her, "Je ne regrette rien.")*

2006

I sit in the garden of the house that I bought as a refugee of my marriage, the house where I lived for a decade with my sons and their other mother, where I have now lived for a decade without my children, but with the love of my life. I watch a hummingbird suck the sweetness from a siren-red blossom. I hear a baby cry—the baby of the Chinese couple next door. Her mother comforts her in a language I do not speak, a language I do understand. The soothing sounds. The baby's sudden silence. The hummingbird's beak plunges into the next flower's center. Sated, or just restless, the hummingbird flits away.

I wish I could say what my lover says. But *je regrette beaucoup.* Despite her longing for motherhood, my lover doesn't know how lucky she is, in this way at least. The dialect of *no regrets* is a language that no mother—*especially a mother who has divorced her children's father*—is ever allowed to speak.

I cannot shrug off my regrets, my mistakes. My sons' backs are bent with their weight. They carried that load from their mom's house to their dad's every Sunday night of their childhoods; they carry it as the fine young men they are, still. The choices I made—to marry their father, to have children with him, to fight to stay in love with him, to lose that fight, to give it up, to leave—have worked out well, for me. I have two brilliant sons, a radiant lover. All I'm missing is the primal dream: *a family, the way it's supposed to be.* The smile exchanged over the child's head from the woman whose body once contained that child, to the man who put that baby there.

He says "hospital" now, but remember how he said "hostibul" till he was six? Who knew, when we gave him a camera for his tenth birthday, that he'd be shooting magazine covers when he was twenty-five? Let's throw him a graduation party; let's pay for the wedding; let's offer to take the grandkids for a week.

Je regrette beaucoup. What could I have done, what should I have done, what didn't I do to make the dream come true? Was there a seed I could have planted, a weed I could have pulled: the day I met my kids' father, the first time I let myself think *I don't want him anymore,* the day I said, *There's nothing more we can do?*

What bad things would my sons have learned, growing up in a miserable marriage, that they haven't learned, growing up in a miserable divorce?

What good things will they learn, raising their children in our patched-together family, that they wouldn't have learned, raising their kids with their father and me? *"This is your grandma, your grandma's wife, your grandpa, your grandpa's domestic partner, your half-uncle, your stepcousin, your godfather-in-law. . . . It's complicated, yes. But so is being human. And that's what being a family means."*

2006

My younger son and his fiancée surprise me at dinnertime: ring the doorbell, shoo me upstairs, tell my lover, "Don't let Mom come down." We hear them giggling, moving chairs, opening and closing doors. They call up to us to ask where the Scotch tape is. They call to us, finally, to come down. They put their hands over my eyes, their arms around my shoulders. They shuffle me through the house.

"Okay, open!" my son says, sounding as excited as he did when he still said "hostibul," but who's here to remember that with me now? He's making new memories with the girl he described to me, the day they met one year ago, as the woman of his dreams.

The kitchen is bobbling with balloons. My son and his beloved have taped them to the counters, to the serving platters, to the cookbooks, to the walls. The table is sprinkled with multicolored foil "Happy Birthday" confetti. A single white candle flickers on a dark chocolate cake, throwing dancing shadows across the floor.

My son and his fiancée stand hip-to-hip, shoulder-to-shoulder, entwined like vines growing up around each other, as if they're one being, or want to be. "Make a wish," my son says, smiling at me. I look at the two of them: faces shining, already so wounded and yet so trusting, so sweet, so beautiful, so new.

May your children sit at this table someday, I pray. *And may they feel that they are in a family, and that their family holds them tight.*

"Blow, Mom!" my son commands me.

And may the damage stop here.

I follow my son's orders. My son, his lover, and my lover clap and cheer. We take our places at the table, in the same four chairs that have always been there. My lover hands me the cake knife we bought for our wedding. They sing "Happy Birthday" to me. I cut the first piece.

"We're so sorry we can't be at your party," my son's fiancée says, her third apology since they told me last week that they had long-standing, unchangeable plans. I clutch my heart in not-so-mock despair. "I'll get through it without you two somehow."

"Aren't you over that yet?" my son asks with not-so-mock impatience.

"I never get over anything," I say. "As you well know."

My son is suddenly serious. "If you never learn how to get over what hurts you," he says, "how will I?"

1996–2006

My new love and I spent every moment of our first three weeks together, marooned on the lush, moist island of our borrowed Berkeley hills bed. But then came the cruel ending of our idyll: her return to her country, a continent and an ocean away.

Already it had all been decided. *You're the one,* she had said to me. *You're the one,* I had said to her. But our last night together she said or did something—*what was it? I can't think when I'm yelling*—that somehow proved her unreliable, unloving, not *the one* I believed her to be. So on the very last night of our very first time together, we had a terrible fight. *I had a fight, that is.* My love sat silently, watching, as I yelled and spun around the room.

"I knew it was too good to be true," I shouted.

"It *is* true," she said, quietly, certainly.

I stopped in the center of the room where I'd set up my base of operations. The mortars were loaded, the cannons aimed at her. I raised my hand, signaled the troops to hold their fire.

"You don't have to shout," she said. "I'm listening. I'll always listen to you."

Always? How can she say that word? Because she's my dream come true? Or because she's a liar, my worst enemy?

"I'll love you forever," she said. And in that moment the world tilted on its axis, and for no reason that I could name, I believed that what she was saying was true.

I believed her. I believed myself.

And so we went on. Six months later she left her country and moved in with me. With me and my raging teenage son, who, when she said, "Don't talk to your mother that way," told her, "It might have been better if you'd raised me, but you didn't, so you can't tell me what to do."

I thought that fight, that night, was the beginning of our ending, the end of our unbelievable—*it was unbelievable, but then I believed it*—beginning. We wouldn't have—*I wouldn't have*—needed to fight if I'd known that the opposite was true.

How can I explain that moment, that certainty, the ten years I have lived since that night without ever once thinking, *She's a liar, she's my enemy, this is too good to be true;* without ever once having to keep myself from thinking *I don't want her anymore?* Is it magic, are we lucky, is it because that night of our first fight—*my last fight*—we drew a circle around ourselves—*she drew a circle around us*—and called it "forever," and both of us promised to stay inside?

Maybe my divorces taught me what matters and what does not; what will keep us inside the circle, what would cause one or both of us to step out. It *is* magic, we *are* lucky: she delights me frequently, annoys me almost never. Still, we are human, and so there are things she says and does that would have sparked fighting words—*that made me yell and scream fighting words*—in every relationship I've been in before.

But somehow even the thing that bothers me most, her smoking—*she's going to die, she's going to leave me*—doesn't spark fighting words now. (*Sickened by the smell of cigarettes as I walk through our front door, by my anger, by my fear, I go from "Honey, I'm home" to fury in two seconds flat. I glare at her, mustering the troops, pointing the cannons. And then I think,* What is it that I'm about to do? Threaten our happiness now, as if that will keep her from dying and leaving me later?)

My lover and I were in the center of our lives when we met. We've both been dancing now—with others, with ourselves, with each other—a long time. We spin each other tenderly, lift each other with strong arms, catch each other with tenderness, but with precision too. If any couple could be invincible it would be us, but we're grateful, not foolish: we know that even our magic, our luck, our hard-won wisdom cannot protect us if we slip, if we slide, if we fail to protect ourselves. We've both stood alone, dazed in the rubble. We know the stage we are dancing on could collapse if we come down on it too hard. We know we are inventing our own pas de deux with each step we take. And so we dance on, with wild abandon.

And with terrible care.

18.
This Old House **Rebecca Barry**

It was winter in upstate New York and I felt like a character in a Russian novel. My husband, nine-month-old son, and I were living with my unmarried sister and three cats in the back three rooms of our 4,500-square-foot brick house because that was the only part of the house we could afford to heat. Everyone had colds and bad tempers. My sister and I were bickering daily. My husband felt he was the only one who ever did the dishes, and the cats kept vomiting on the rug. Even the baby was tired of our life. One morning he crawled out into the kitchen/living room/playroom, looked at the beige walls, looked at his toys, and let out a howl of despair.

How this happened goes something like this: Tommy and I decided to follow a dream. We both loved old houses and had always wanted to fix one up, so we put our house in Columbus, Ohio, on the market and bought an "as is" brick Italianate building built in 1865 in a small town in upstate New York. We chose upstate New York because my parents live there and could babysit, and also because I grew up there and love the landscape: the acres of farmland, the

Greek Revival farmhouses, the miles of creek. We chose our house because it was beautiful and had character and rental income, and was also within walking distance of a post office, espresso shop, the drugstore, and a bar with live music, as well as open fields and woodland. Our realtor, my sister, swore it was a good choice. A great investment.

Then she quit her job as a realtor and moved in with us to work as a live-in nanny in exchange for rent. Which just goes to show you should always check your realtor's references.

I'll admit I had a fantasy about my whole extended family somehow living together in this house. The place had been originally built as a duplex, and while it was now divided into six apartments, I imagined that we could eventually take most of them over. As a child I had loved books like *All-of-a-Kind Family* and *Return to Gone-Away Lake,* where families and sometimes extended families occupied the same building, or a rambling house in a beautiful place became as much of a part of the family as the people who lived in it. And I've always been drawn to houses full of people. I love the company, the shared space, the mishmash of music and meals that living with people makes. So when I looked at this huge house with its hand-hewn moldings, six furnaces, twenty-one rooms, three sunporches, and something like six bathrooms, I thought, We could all live here. And then have even more space to rent out to artists and musicians, and I would have a house full of family and music and art, and my children would be raised by a rich, collective community. And since there were six kitchens, people wouldn't even have to share kitchen space, which we all know leads to violence.

By midwinter, however, I began to realize that there were a few teeny, tiny problems with my plans.

One: we had no money for renovation. Motherhood was cutting into my work time, my husband's job was only part-time, and with two mortgages (our house in Columbus still hadn't sold), we were hemorrhaging savings. I was waiting for my husband to sit me down and say, "Darling, it's over. We're *ruined*."

Two: while we both loved the idea of fixing up a house, it turned out that both of us secretly thought the other one would make all the phone calls.

Three: although we had begun the extended family living situation by inviting my sister to live with us and help us with child care in exchange for low rent, my sister and I were about to kill each other.

This wasn't entirely new for us. Part of our closeness as siblings came from the ways we tried to take care of each other, which usually involved telling each other what to do, and which for some reason we always took personally. (So *surprising*! Especially since we usually prefaced our bossiness with "Don't take this personally." "Don't take this personally," I'd say. "Do you have to keep taking antidepressants?" "Don't take this personally," she'd say. "But maybe book-writing just isn't for you right now.")

Perhaps you can see the problem.

We were also both in difficult places in our lives. My sister had just turned forty and had had a minor breakdown in

D.C., where she'd been living. She'd quit her job working as a union organizer and had come home with no other plan than to be near family. She was working low-paying, part-time jobs, not sure what to do with her life, but certain that she did want a husband and a baby.

At thirty-seven, I had a husband and a baby, but while I loved my new son more than I could bear, I wasn't so happy with being a mother. I didn't have much patience, and couldn't stand the sleep deprivation. And I very much wanted to get back to work. I felt invisible as a mother, like the big piece of myself the world used to see was gone. So there was an unspoken power struggle going on between my sister and me. I resented feeling like I had to take care of her, but I liked, for once in my life, being in a position of power in our relationship. She resented being treated like a child, but, at this moment in her life, really needed some help.

So we would fight. At first we fought over big things—money, drinking habits, child care—but it wasn't long before just the littlest thing would set us off. A typical evening conversation might go something like this. My sister, husband, and I would be sitting in the common room. Maria would be playing a game on my computer. I'd be annoyed because when I'd come home to an empty house the day before, the heat and lights had been on. I'd assume Maria was the one who left them on, and would be furious, as my husband and I were paying for heat and electricity. I wouldn't want to start a fight, though, so I'd talk about a song I'd heard on the radio. And a conversation like this would ensue:

Me: You know that song "Wildwood Flower"? From that Carter Family album we used to listen to? I heard it on the radio today.

Maria: I can't stand that song.

Me: What? How can you say that? It's the exact same tune as "Honky Tonk Angels," and you love that song.

Maria: That's completely different.

Me: No it isn't. Listen. (I sing "Wildwood Flower.")

Maria: Right. It's so boring. There's no chorus.

Me: What are you talking about? I just sang the chorus!

Maria: When was the last time you heard it?

Me: I listen to it all the time!

Maria: No, I mean the other song.

Me: I'm telling you, it's the same song.

Tommy: So what! Why can't a person like "Baa, Baa, Black Sheep" and dislike "Twinkle, Twinkle, Little Star"?

Silence.

Me: Why do you even play that stupid computer game?

Maria: Why are you so annoying?

Me: Did you leave the lights on yesterday?

You get the picture. It was a rocky period for all of us.

We were also developing an uneasy relationship with the house. The roof leaked, and there was a ten-inch slant to the floors and a huge bulge in the plaster in the front hallway. One night when I was taking a shower, my husband, who was in the living room, heard dripping and found a deluge of water coming from the ceiling in the back. Water was puddling on the floor, leaking onto the built-in cabinets and a light switch. He yelled and I came downstairs in my towel, looked at the mess, figured it would cost about a million dollars, and started to cry.

We called my father, who's done a lot of work on old houses. He said it might cost a lot, but maybe not. His own father had a shower in the guest room that if you stood in a certain way leaked all over the piano in the living room. Every time this happened, my grandfather would grab a broomstick he kept by the piano music, bang on the ceiling, and yell at the guest to move to the left. And that cost him nothing.

This began a discussion about where I was standing when I was in the shower and I admitted that there was water all over the floor when I was done showering, nothing unusual, and then my sister pointed out that when she'd taken a shower there had been no deluge. It turned out that the real problem with the shower was me, because at the age of thirty-seven, I still hadn't learned that the shower curtain goes inside the tub. (We had a bathtub with no shower when I was growing up. Sue me.)

Then, a few weeks later, I put my foot through our bedroom ceiling while my husband was trying to sleep.

When you have an infant, sleep becomes a currency unlike anything else your marriage has seen. Nothing is worse than not getting enough sleep. You age. Your whole personality changes. The slightest mishap can throw you into a vitriolic rage. Once my husband came home and took a nap without asking me, and I almost dumped a diaper pail on his head.

The morning I put my foot through the ceiling, I had offered to take the baby because my husband was up late working and I was trying to be a good wife. (An idea that almost always backfires—trying to be a good wife.) One of the cats got into the attic, which meant she was going to pee on something, so I hauled Liam upstairs and while I was holding my son and yelling at the cat, I misstepped and put my foot through the attic floor.

I heard my husband say, "What the hell?" and went downstairs, where he was in bed, covered with insulation, wood splinters, and Sheetrock.

"Sorry," I said.

My husband pulled the covers over his head, told me to take the cat to the pound, and shut the bedroom door. Then he went back to sleep, insulation and lath clinging to his hair.

A few days, later Tommy went to New York on business for a week and as soon as he was out the door, Liam got a fever and an earache. He was burning up and inconsolable and I was trying to soothe him when my sister came in and said she couldn't babysit in the afternoon like she'd agreed to, because she hadn't gotten done everything she'd wanted to do the day before and needed time to finish it. I was furious. I had been up all night and was exhausted and I couldn't believe how selfish she was being. She couldn't believe how rigid I was being, and noted that every time my husband left, instead of getting mad at him, I got mad at her.

I told her she took too much medication.

She told me I needed some.

I told her she was unreliable.

She told me I was a hard person to work for. (Her exact words for "hard person" might have been "mean bitch.")

The baby started crying. My sister and I started yelling.

She told me to fire her.

I told her she was fired.

She quit.

The baby began howling and pulling his ears as if we were literally hurting his head.

My sister went off to her room, which was in the prettiest part of the building. (Which just goes to show that no matter how old you are, and even if you own the house, your sister somehow still gets the nicest room.)

I stood in my bedroom, kissing Liam's burning head, wiping away my own hot, angry tears, wondering why my sister and I even bothered trying. We were so different. In fact, if we weren't sisters, we probably wouldn't even be friends. In my mind, she *never* changed her behavior just to make other people happy. I *always* did, to the point where I was sometimes untrue to myself.

I sat in bed and looked up at my ceiling with the huge hole in it, missing my husband but thinking that if he were home I'd probably be fighting with him too. I was so tired. And screwed, because I had just fired my nanny and had no babysitting tomorrow and would probably be up all night with a sick child again.

How did I end up here? I thought. And why did I ever think any of this was a good idea?

. . .

But I know why I'd thought it was a good idea. There are advantages to family living together as adults. My sister and I loved each other. In spite of our fighting, we liked being in the same house, being able to pop into each other's apartments for a drink or to see if the other wanted to get coffee. And who we are in our families is often who we are in the world—the little sister always trying to catch up, the older brother trying to take care of everything, trying to smooth things over, the baby who feels left out and wants so desperately to be heard. If we're going to manage the difficult situations we recreate in the outside world, it helps to start reconfiguring our roles within the family. And in many ways, choosing to live with each other as grown-ups forces you to do this, and to work out things you might otherwise simply avoid.

The next day, my sister offered to help me with the baby, but also asked if I would be willing to see a counselor with her. She said that our fights were too personal, too frequent. She was worried that if we didn't get help, we might stop speaking to each other altogether. I knew what she meant. I was worried about the same thing. I looked at her, standing there in our kitchen, my baby in her arms. I felt that tug I always feel around my older sister, of wanting to be next to her as much as I want to be able to pull away, of wanting her approval, of wanting her to be different and yet exactly the same, of loving her so much and never knowing how to say it.

So we went to couples therapy.

Our counselor was named Theresa—a petite woman with long white hair and kind eyes. I have met only one other person in my life like Theresa, a surgeon named Yasmin. Both of these women exude such a sense of compassion and wisdom and warmth that you want them to move in with you and advise you for the rest of your life. When she first met Liam, Yasmin took his hand in hers and said, "Hello, Liam. My name is Yasmin, and this is my house, where I live with my husband, who is also my friend. And this is the cherry tree that lives in my front yard and makes me happy each morning when I look at it. Do you like it? Here. I'll give you one of its blossoms. Normally, I like the flowers on the tree, but since you are a special guest, I will give this to you as a present."

The boy melted in her hands.

I felt that way around Theresa. She had a gentle, soft-spoken manner, and a way of normalizing our frailties without triggering defensiveness.

"What are your fights about?" she asked us when we came in and sat down.

"She says I'm inflexible," I said.

"Are you?" she said. "That's not always a bad thing."

It was as if she had given me a Xanax. (Well, maybe half of one.) It had never occurred to me that it was all right to be inflexible at times (which often got me into trouble because I would pretend I was cool and easygoing about things I didn't want to do and then resent it later).

"Are you unreliable?" she said to Maria a few minutes later.

"I don't think so," my sister said. I looked at her as if she had grown a goiter. She looked back at me as if to say, What is your problem?

"Not in my professional life," she said. Then she added, "I guess I tend to be more unreliable with my sister."

"Great," said Theresa. "So maybe we can look at whether it's reasonable for her to ask you for help."

"She just makes you feel like all of your faults are normal," I said to my husband later.

"That's a nice quality," he said. We were lying in bed, having just had sex because a friend of mine had said that when you're living in a chaotic house and you've just put your foot through the ceiling and you're in therapy with your sister, you need to have sex with your husband to relieve all the tension. It's good advice, and seemed to have worked.

"What does she want you to do about it?" he said.

I explained the techniques Theresa had given us: make clear, written agreements about rent, hours for child care, and food. Ask each other if we wanted the other's opinion before offering it. When we felt our fights slipping into that old familiar pattern where everything was personal and one or both of us was turning mean, we were to stop the fight and make an appointment to revisit it the next day.

"That's the part I hate," I said. The day before, I'd been on the phone with a friend of mine and heard myself say, "I have to go. I have an appointment with my sister to talk about what an asshole I am."

But as irritating and sometimes infantilizing as our homework seemed, slowly my relationship with my sister began to shift. Our fights, while still frequent, were shorter. What had taken us three hours to sort through before therapy was now taking about half an hour.

And we slowly, very slowly, stopped having to be right, which is shockingly hard to do.

One of the things that struck me in therapy was the way my sister and I heard things differently. I would think I said, "If your boyfriend doesn't want children, maybe you shouldn't keep seeing him," and she would hear, "You're doing everything wrong." Or sometimes she would say she was angry because I'd told her to shut up in an argument, and I would swear that she was the one who said that to me. Who knows who was right? Most of us are moving through the world experiencing things completely differently, thinking that we're on the same page. Given this, it's amazing that any of us get along at all. And if you're trying to live together, maybe the point is not to prove whose view is right or wrong, but to figure out how to navigate our relationships with the assumption that most of us have good intentions and are at least trying not to hurt each other. Which is also shockingly hard to do.

Not long after we'd started implementing our homework, my sister and I were in therapy talking about a pile of food bills that were sitting in a box on a shelf in the kitchen.

Someone needed to go through them to see who owed what for food, and while my husband and I kept meaning to do it, we never seemed to have enough time. Theresa asked if it was something Maria could do, and she said she didn't have a lot of time either. "Dividing up bills shouldn't take more than a few hours," said Theresa. "Who do you think has enough time to do it?"

"She does," we both said.

There was a pause. We looked at each other.

"You don't have a *baby*," I said.

"You don't have a *job*," she said.

These were both low blows, since she desperately wanted a baby, and I was spending every free minute on fiction writing, which isn't really considered a job by a lot of people, including me.

"It seems to me like neither of you have much respect for the other's life," Theresa said.

I have since, many times, come back to this moment. Because it's the fundamental respect for each other that keeps any family system, any household system, or any governmental system from falling apart. We weren't treating each other with respect, in part because deep down both of us were so jealous of what the other had. I was jealous of her freedom to come and go as she pleased; she was jealous of my motherhood. And beneath the jealousy was admiration—I admired her ability to say no, her way of beautifying any space she had. She admired my diligence, the way I seemed to get what I wanted.

In fact, none of us were being very respectful of one another at that time. I wasn't necessarily respecting my husband's work, because I was mad that he kept leaving me with the baby to go do it. My husband wasn't respecting how sleep-deprived I was. My sister wasn't respecting my need to write, and I wasn't respecting how worried she was about ever finding a partner. And all of us had been so overwhelmed and complaining so much about the house that we weren't respecting how beautiful it was or how lucky we were to have it.

I read somewhere that Jung said a house is a situation, and this situation reflects your life. The house, with its needy roof, its beautiful tall windows and crown moldings, and the sprinkler system that ran through our living room left over from a brief period when the downstairs was occupied by a store, reflected the way we were all a work in progress. It breathed potential—for itself, for all of us, and for our dreams: my dream of having an unconventional, sprawling family under one roof, my husband's dream of breathing new life into an old place, my sister's dream of having a child. But to achieve new dreams you have to break down your old self, and our house reflected that as well. It was the chaos the flower goes through before it bursts into blossom, the ugliness a teenager goes through before becoming an adult. And with our furniture all over the place and our bedroom in what used to be a kitchen, it was kind of a mess.

Everyone had told us that when you buy a house to fix up, you start with one small corner and make it yours. We looked around. If we did fix the foundation, it would probably mean cracks in the plaster from shifting walls, so whatever work we did before we jacked up the house would be

undone. The front room upstairs, which got the best light
and would make the best bedroom, had no heat. Our son,
Liam, still didn't have a nursery—which wasn't a huge problem since he wouldn't sleep in a crib and spent his nights
hurtling back and forth like a monkey in his baby swing. We
could paint the beige living room/kitchen/playroom, but we
couldn't agree on the color. What part could we make ours?
Why wouldn't our child sleep in a crib like a normal kid? We
didn't know where to begin.

We decided to throw a party.

I've always believed there's nothing like a good party to
make you like your house. I invited everyone—strangers
from the coffee shop, my mother's friends, and a Spanish
artist named Fernando, who happened to be strolling down
the street and said we had a nice house. Then I hired a band
that was playing at the bistro next door once when we were
out for dinner.

The day of the party, I accidentally knocked the bedroom
door off its hinges, and my husband said that our real problem with the place was not lack of money or time or energy,
but that I had the grace of a wildebeest.

We angrily started to clean the house and then it started
to snow and people began calling to say they wouldn't be
able to come. But then a woman I'd met at the coffee shop
arrived with her three-year-old, and my friend Domenica
and her husband brought their friend Hitch, a tall, handsome gardener who knows everyone in town. My sister's ex-
boyfriend, a rocket scientist, arrived with some whiskey
from Prague. Fernando, the Spanish artist, came with his
lady friend, Kim, and my mother brought her friend Carol.

Then the musicians (a banjo player, fiddler, and bassist) showed up and we all began to drink. Snow poured down outside, an impromptu blizzard in March. The musicians started to play and people started to dance. Hitch went to the bar down the street and brought back two more fiddlers.

I drank some vodka and looked out the windows. It was beautiful, with snow clinging to the trees, and the streetlights giving them a soft, purplish hue. Inside, my husband was holding our baby and dancing with my sister, and the woman from the coffee shop was having a firm talk with her three-year-old about eating too much cake. The house seemed alive, healthy; people were singing and laughing while outside the spring snow fell and fell, flirting like mad with the wind.

I knew the next day we'd be back upstairs, circling each other in a miasma of indecision, but in that moment, everything—our house, our new friends, our new life—seemed perfect. The music got louder and people began to move faster, stomping their feet and clapping. I watched my husband spinning around with our baby in his arms, my sister laughing with a man who would later become her husband. She looked so beautiful—flushed, and happy. I thought about how close my sister and I had come to losing each other, and what a terrible sadness that would have been.

We're so lucky, I thought. Look at this rich, full house. We did it. We have everything we ever wanted.

We're home.

And then my husband passed our baby to my sister, and came over to ask me to dance. Like any well-mannered wildebeest, I said yes.

Acknowledgments

Instead of thanks, I should send a first-class, round-trip ticket to the destination of her choice to my editor, Sarah McGrath, and a new PowerBook to her assistant, Sarah Stein. Without their patience and perseverance I would still be at my laptop, polishing another draft of the introduction. They have no idea how much they helped me keep it together during the final days of finishing this manuscript.

Thank you to Geoffrey Kloske, Susan Petersen Kennedy, and Jennifer Rudolph Walsh. I take your firm and steady support seriously. Thank you to the writers included in the book, and the others who wrote their hearts out and went on to pitch their excellent essays to *Vanity Fair, The Sun, Vogue,* and *Harper's.* It was a long and sometimes frustrating process, but you all exhibited nothing but grace and goodwill.

Of course, I must also thank my own families, the one that raised me and the one that keeps me around as long as I stock the kitchen with Tang, organic dark chocolate, Silk soy milk, and root-beer-flavored Popsicles. The truth is, I'm not the easiest family member on the block. I endlessly look for new ways to organize household items, and order depressing foreign films from Netflix. My son thinks my laptop is a third, albeit large and white, hand, and I am either packing a suitcase or unpacking one at all times.

All to say, I'm a very lucky woman. And I know it. And there is no way to thank the people responsible. I'd need at least a hundred lifetimes, and even then, it wouldn't be enough. But you know who you are, and you know what you've done, and I hope you will forgive me for all the things I know I did wrong, and all the things I know I did wrong but don't remember.

As ever, I thank each and every reader of this and my four other books. I never, ever take you for granted.

Credits

"Counting on Cousins" by Amy Anderson. © Amy Anderson.

"Woman Up" by asha bandele. Copyright asha bandele 2009. Appeared in a different form in *Maybe Baby*, ed. Lori Leibovich. Used by permission of the author.

"This Old House" by Rebecca Barry. © Rebecca Barry.

"And Then We Were Poly" by Jenny Block. Copyright Jenny Block 2009. Appeared in a different form in *Tango* magazine.

"Daddy Donoring" by Antonio Caya. © Antonio Caya.

"Sharing Madison" by Dawn Friedman. Copyright Dawn Friedman 2009. Appeared in a different form in Salon.com. Used by permission of the author.

"Unassisted" by Sasha Hom. © Sasha Hom.

"Foreign Relations" by Suzanne Kamata. © Suzanne Kamata.

"Like Family" by Min Jin Lee. © Min Jin Lee.

"Love, Money, and the Unmarried Couple" by Judith Levine. © Judith Levine.

"Till Life Do Us Part" by Meredith Maran. © Meredith Maran.

"Two Red Lines" by Susan McKinney de Ortega. © Susan McKinney de Ortega.

"My First Husband" by Liza Monroy. Copyright Liza Monroy 2009. Appeared in a different form in *Psychology Today*.

257

Credits

About the Contributors

Amy Anderson grew up with five brothers and four sisters in a crowded house, where she learned how to answer random questions about international adoption and cook dinner for twelve using ingredients from the Canned Food Outlet. She is the cofounder and coeditor of mamazine.com, and lives in California with her husband, three children, and an endlessly rotating clan of extended family, including cousins.

asha bandele is the author of five books, including the award-winning bestseller *The Prisoner's Wife*. Her second memoir, *Something Like Beautiful: One Single Mother's Story*, is forthcoming from Bloomsbury. She lives in Brooklyn with her daughter, Nisa.

Rebecca Barry is the author of the novel in stories *Later, at the Bar*, a New York Times Notable Book and a New York Times Editors' Choice. Her nonfiction has appeared in many publications, including *Hallmark*, *Real Simple*, the *Washington Post Magazine*, the *New York Times*, and *Best American Travel Writing* (2003). She currently lives in upstate New York with her husband and two sons, whom she writes about on her blog, The Main Street Diaries, http://mainstreetdiaries.blog spot.com.

Jenny Block is the author of the memoir *Open: Love, Sex, and Life in an Open Marriage*. Her work has appeared in *Tango*, the *Huffington Post, ElleGirl, Literary Mama*, and the collections *It's a Girl: Women Writers on Raising Daughters* and *Letters to My Teacher*. She has been married to her husband, Christopher, for eleven years and seeing her girlfriend, Jemma, for two; Christopher and Jenny have a nine-year-old daughter named Emily.

Antonio Caya is a pseudonym for a very happy donor who wishes to remain anonymous to protect the feelings of all involved, both young and old.

Dawn Friedman is the owner of openbookstrategies.com, a Web 2.0 marketing company for writers. Her essays have appeared in *Parenting, WonderTime, Brain Child, Bitch, Adoptive Families, Utne Reader,* and *Salon*. Her blog about open adoption, www.thiswomanswork.com, was featured in *Time* magazine. She is currently working on a memoir about her life with Madison.

Sasha Hom is a Korean adoptee raised by a Chinese-American family in Berkeley, California. She temporarily resides in Davis, California, where she is working on a book about her experiences living nomadically in a one-ton veggie-oil van. To read her journal and keep track of her journey, visit www.sashahom.com.

Suzanne Kamata is the author of the novel *Losing Kei*. She is the editor of the anthology *Love You to Pieces: Creative Writers on Raising a Child with Special Needs*, the fiction editor at literarymama.com, and a five-time Pushcart Prize nominee. She lives on the island of Shikoku in Japan with her husband, twins, and mother-in-law.

Min Jin Lee is the author of the novel *Free Food for Millionaires*, a national bestseller, No. 1 Book Sense Pick, New York Times Editors' Choice, and Wall Street Journal Book Club selection. She has received the New York Foundation for the Arts Fellowship for Fiction, the Peden Prize from the Missouri Review for Best Story, and the Narrative Prize for New and Emerging Writers. She lives in Tokyo with her husband and son and is working on her second novel, *Pachinko*.

Judith Levine's work explores the ways culture, politics, and the marketplace are entwined in intimate life. She is the author of four books, including *Harmful to Minors*, which won the Los Angeles Times Book Prize, and, most recently, *Not Buying It: My Year Without Shopping*. Her award-winning column, "Poli Psy," appears in the Vermont weekly *Seven Days*.

Meredith Maran is an award-winning journalist and the author of several nonfiction books, including *Dirty: America's Teenage Drug Epidemic* and *Class Dismissed: A Year in the Life of an American High School*. She writes for *Playboy*, *Salon*, *Real Simple*, *More*, *Vibe*, *Family Circle*, and other magazines, and is currently at work on a novel about a gorgeous bisexual. She lives in Oakland, California, with her wife, the horticultural genius Katrine Thomas.

Susan McKinney de Ortega lives in San Miguel de Allende, where she and her husband own Jasmine Spa and her two daughters ride dressage and attend a bilingual middle school based in transcendental meditation. She is currently working on a memoir about her life as the expatriate daughter of a basketball coach. Her house now includes a bedroom for her daughters.

Liza Monroy is the author of a novel, *Mexican High*. She is at work on her next book, which expands on—and digresses from—her essay in this collection. She lives in Brooklyn, teaches writing at Columbia University, and is still best friends with Razi.

ZZ Packer is a Jones Lecturer at Stanford University. Her stories have appeared in *The New Yorker, Harper's, Story*, and several anthologies, including *The Best American Short Stories of 2000*. Her collection of short stories, *Drinking Coffee Elsewhere,* was published by Riverhead Books.

Paula Penn-Nabrit, J.D., was baptized at the Church of Christ Apostolic Faith and received the Holy Ghost five years later. She graduated from the Columbus School for Girls, Wellesley College, and the Ohio State University College of Law. She is married to the fabulously enigmatic Charles Nabrit, and is the president of the international management consulting firm PN&A.

Neal Pollack, the author of several semi-acclaimed books of fiction and nonfiction, lives in Los Angeles with his wife, Regina Allen, and their six-year-old son, Elijah. He's writing a book about yoga. God help us all.

Dan Savage is the award-winning author of the internationally syndicated sex-advice column "Savage Love" and the editor of *The Stranger*, Seattle's weekly newspaper. His writing has appeared in the *New York Times Magazine*, the op-ed pages of the *New York Times, Rolling Stone, The Onion*, and other publications. This essay is excerpted from his book *The Commitment: Love, Sex, Marriage and My Family*.

Marc and Amy Vachon are the founders of the website equallysharedparenting.com, which was featured in the *New York Times*, the *Boston Globe*, the *Washington Post*, and on *The Today Show*. They live in Massachusetts with their six-year-old daughter and three-year-old son, and are currently writing a book about the benefits and challenges of creating an egalitarian family life.